TEACHING ENGLISH IN SECONDARY SCHOOLS

TEACHING ENGLISH IN SECONDARY SCHOOLS

B.V. VERGHESE

ANMOL PUBLICATIONS PVT. LTD.
NEW DELHI - 110 002 (INDIA)

ANMOL PUBLICATIONS PVT. LTD.
4374/4B, Ansari Road, Daryaganj
New Delhi - 110 002
Ph.: 23261597, 23278000
Visit us: www.anmolpublications.com

Teaching English in Secondary Schools

ISBN 81-7488-982-5

PRINTED IN INDIA

Published by J.L. Kumar for Anmol Publications Pvt. Ltd., New Delhi - 110 002 and Printed at Mehra Offset Press, Delhi.

Contents

Preface

'Teaching' i.e. 'effective teaching' is a complex and distinct art. With the change in time and circumstances 'teaching-learning' process has also changed tremendously. English Language teaching especially requires special skill.

The present work, in five volumes, is designed to equip teachers and students with Modern Methods of teaching English. Volume-wise organisation of the work is: Teaching English as a Bilingual Language; Teaching of General English; Teaching English in Elementary Schools; Teaching English in Secondary Schools; and Creativity in English Language Teaching. As is obvious from the names this work will prove a veritable mine of information.

The editor acknowledges his gratefulness to all learned writers whose writings are cited or substantially made use of in the present work. Constructive suggestions for improvement of the work from the learned readers are welcome.

B. V. Verghese

1

Literature in the Secondary School: Plan and Materials

WE pass now, after our rapid survey of general literary aims, ethical and practical, during the four years of the Secondary School, to a consideration of the details of the work and the stages of progression.

As to the beginnings, experience in teaching both the higher Grammar Grades and Secondary School Freshmen, has borne in upon us the importance of investing the Secondary School period with distinctive character, — of fostering in the freshman a strong sense of the new page turned, the new chapter begun, the fresh start, the new opportunity. This result will to some extent come of itself. The freshman feels at once, by the less regimental treatment, the larger trust, the expectation of stricter self-government, that he has advanced a step toward the life of freedom. The organization of the studies under a body of specialists is an intimation that higher and more exacting work is to be required of him. The appearance of the elective factor — in the matter of foreign languages at any rate (we will not gnaw here at this scarred bone of contention) — brings with it thoughts of a life- career which give a new sense of nearness to manhood's responsibilities.

We believe in utilizing this factor in the English work. Let us signalize this new departure. We have found a certain virtue in using the term Rhetoric in conjunction with our Composition, just to give the sense of *a terra incognita;* of a new outlook on the composition work from a more commanding elevation. We have avoided Grammar if our freshmen have had a strong, recent dose of it. We have tried to strike a new vein of interest in the reading matter, and to indicate that we are taking a step forward in our methods of study. Our first written exercise has been a series of questions as to previous work in English, — books read in and out of school, the part reading has played in the student's life, his preferences, and how they have changed, etc. This inventory is, for many reasons, an invaluable document: and until it is received, all plans for the year's work must be to some extent provisional. The wise teacher will not be satisfied with it alone. He will get all available information concerning the schools from which his students have come, and the course of English study pursued there.

Following the same cue, and realizing the importance of beginnings in all things, the teacher will be careful to plan certain typical lessons and experiences for the newcomers, which shall suggest the spirit and the atmosphere that is to surround the work. There is to be enlarged recognition of individual rights and responsibilities, to meet the growth of the feeling of realized selfhood that is proper to the adolescent period. Each pupil will be gently thrown back upon himself by being asked at an early moment to do an individual piece of work — report to his class on this or that matter.

Again, because this period is marked by a greater capacity of intellectual labour and concentrated attention, the first tasks will announce to the class that more prolonged and more absorbed effort is to be exacted of them. But this severer effort is to be made in an air of quiet, promoting an eager yet tranquil activity. For it is a peculiarity of adolescent period that, while the pulse of life beat strong, while vitality is at the flood and emotion is often torrential, there is great danger of overstimulating and overtaxing. This new life, while it must find sufficient outlet, must also be husbanded. "Inspire enthusiastic activity, " is the safest motto for the teacher at this time, counsels Dr. Stanley Hall; but he is also very insistent that we must avoid a prodigal employment of this " new and final invoice of energy." It is the more necessary to conduct the work in a spirit of glad yet quiet diligence, because these young men and women (notably the young women) are subject, many of them, to moods or spells, now of inertia, and now of unwonted activity; of elation, and depression (thoughts of suicide are not uncommon at this time, we are told). So that we shall aim in these first recitations and meetings with our freshmen to strike the key-note of dignified and tranquil, yet inspiring and laborious effort. We are going to work for the sake of the joy in the work, yet sometimes grimly against the grain for ends to be taken on trust.

With such thoughts in our minds, we shall be careful to choose promising reading matter to make a start with, preferably two or three short selections in poetry and prose; following a rule — to be observed through the Secondary School course — of sandwiching the quieter books judiciously among the more exciting ones. These " points of rest" give a happy rhythm to the work. After the stir and tension of works like " The Ancient Mariner," "The Tale of Two Cities, " " Julius Caesar." " Macbeth," let us have the contrasting calm of " The Deserted Village" or Gray's "Elegy," of Lamb or Hawthorne, of Sir Roger and Mr. Spectator and the Rev. Dr. Primrose.

What particular works we select for our first year students will depend largely upon our general scheme for the four years. The simplest scheme is that which adapts itself in part to the composition work. In the first year a generous proportion of the books will be of the narrative order; in the second, following the change of emphasis in the composition work, descriptive literature will receive special attention; while masterpieces of exposition and argument will claim attention in the third and fourth years. But it is one thing to allow a certain emphasis to fall, now upon narrative, and now upon descriptive literature and so on, following the composition work; quite another to confine attention almost exclusively in any year to one or the other order. In the first place, — repeating our argument in Chapter XI,— the student is concerned in his varied daily work with all forms of composition; secondly, there is no principle of logical progression that either binds the different kinds of writing together in a given sequence, or clearly separates them, — at least, this is true of narration and description, which overlap ; thirdly, we need some variety for the sake of the varied interests and quick contemporaneous developments of the adolescent period; fourthly, the mind does not develop in any such linear fashion, but is advancing in the sum of its powers, including the reasoning and argumentative powers, the recognition of which we so often delay until the third or fourth year; lastly, the scheme is too long drawn out and monotonous, — an objection that applies with special force to a year's occupation with description and the descriptive type of literary masterpiece. We should as little think of prescribing for each of the four years an exclusive study of the novel, the eqic, the essay, and the speech respectively. We rather recommend a scheme that includes in each year's work most of the leading types of literary art, with intensive, emphasized work (correlating with the composition, — where, however, we must equally avoid monotony) during part of the year in one direction. Thus, we should feed and develop the various powers of the mind, — inventional, constructive, imaginative, observational, reasoning, and persuasive, — while these would receive each in its turn that intensive, systematic, analytical treatment that gives to the student the self-conscious mastery of them.

Our first year's course will, then, take shape after this fashion. Emphasis at the outset will be upon narrative literature, and for these reasons : it gives a wholesome objective bias to the work; it carries over the tendencies of what we have called the epic phase of the higher Grammar Grades into the incipient stage of the adolescent period, before many of the students have reached the age of puberty ; and it enables us to settle down to the large structural aspects and problems that are basic in advanced literary studies. We shall deal with the ballad, expanding into the short epic, noting the difference between the lyric and the epic mode; and with the short story, leading us on to the novel, noting the differences between these two species upon which Professor Brander Matthews has insisted in his "Philosophy of the Short Story." We shall not attempt to go far into theory at this stage -- only so far as will enable the student to appreciate more keenly the excellences of the typical masterpieces he is reading. This work will find its natural complement in the study of a play by Shakespeare, the emphasis being distributed between the structural and poetic features and the character interest of the play.

As to the works to be selected for these varied studies, we shall be guided by what our freshman class has read. If they have not taken Scott, we may use him, — a ballad, an epic, a novel. Rossetti's ballad of "The White Ship," and Arnold's "Sohrab and Rustum" or "Balder Dead," among the shorter epics, are especially suitable. We have found few things better than the parts of the "Odyssey" (in Bryant's version), brought together in No. 43 of the Riverside Literature series, under the title "Ulysses among the Phaeacians," which can be timed for the moment when the class is busy in its history work with the early Greek period. The relation of the ballad to the epic may be brought out strikingly in dealing with Homer ; and a ballad or lyric treatment of some of the episodes that are included in our selection may be used for comparative purposes. The story of the "Odyssey" as a whole also gives us a chance to work in some of the loveliest of lyrics on classic themes, — Tennyson's "Lotos Eaters," Dobson's "Prayer of the Swine to Circe," and many other stories which the teacher will find in Gayley's indispensable "Classic Myths in English Literature" (Ginn) . What task can be more stimulating to the teacher than that of bringing his students, at such a critical transitional moment in their lives, into touch with Homer and the noble simplicity of the Homeric world ; — with Ulysses at his best ; with the athletic youth of Phaeacia; with the magical grace of Nausicaa's robust young womanhood; with the refined simplicity of the royal household of Arete, and the chaste beauty of Phaeacia's craftsmanship and life ?

Also as to the short story and the novel, we shall draw upon Hawthorne or Poe, Irving ("Tales of a Traveller" preferably), Kipling, Scott, Stevenson, Dickens, or Thackeray, according to the conditions by which we find ourselves confronted.

In addition to this study of the narrative poem in association with the ballad, and of the short story leading on to the novel and the play, we shall make room for a generous supply of lyric poetry, and the beginnings of public speaking and debate. In the Secondary School no less than in the Elementary School, much lyric poetry would be learned, and sung or recited, in connection with the commemorations and festivals, the morning exercises, and the entertainments given by the school. On this head we must refer to our general treatment of the matter in Chapter X.

The work in public speaking and debate should be the beginning of a course that is to be carried through the four years of the Secondary School : and it will be convenient to outline it at this point. An interest in debating will have manifested itself doubtless — at least on the boys' part — in the upper Grammar Grades; and some teachers have successfully organized work in debating there. The zest is often keen in the Secondary School freshmen. We should gratify it informally at first, and make our beginning , as part of the work in composition, with the writing and delivery of short speeches of a commemorative rather than of an argumentative character. Lincoln's Gettysburg Speech will give us an initial impulse, the student trying his hand at brief orations for use at the Thanksgiving Day or Memorial Day exercises, or short eulogies for Washington's or Lincoln's Birthday. Other types of short speeches — the complimentary speech suitable to the class-gathering or surprise-party, the birthday celebration, or what not — may be worked in. This may be made valuable in developing a sense of differences in literary tone and style — in literary pitch; and it will give steadiness and address in platform work, and impart a touch of reality and immediacy to the literary studies.

In the second and third years this work in oratory and debate may be carried steadily forward into the field of argument, the school debating club being utilized as an indispensable annex; and in the fourth year it may find its culmination in connection with the study of Burke's Speech on Conciliation, required, as it fortunately happens, for collage entrance. The studies would aim at the development of the reasoning powers, would involve an elementary study of logic, and would centre in the preparation of the notes and briefs to be used in speech-making. The student would be taught haw to work up topics, and how to apply, in a new way and with obvious exigency, the principles of literary construction (unity, clearness, coherence, repetition, summary, illustration, figures, climax, etc.) which he has previously seen in relation to the narrative and the description. It is remarkable how much these are vitalized by the needs of the debate. In the third year there might be valuable intensive work on Webster.[1] The teacher will find many available cheap texts that will furnish material from which the student will be able to draw much nutritive thought, and catch the glow of an ardent patriotism and humanitarianism : Lincoln's and Washington's Speeches, Schurz's Eulogy of Lincoln's, Webster's Speeches, and some of Emerson's and Lowell's Addresses, in the Riverside series; Curtis on the Public Duty of Educated Men, some of the Campaign Speeches of Lincoln and Douglas, etc., in Maynard's English Classic Series.

How much time should be spared for this work must depend upon the teacher's power and equipment, and upon the school conditions. It might be made an elective, and an adjunct of the debating club. We have known it to be worked in as a

---

1. An admirable Text-book would be Professor F. V. Scott's edition of some of Webster's Speeches in Longmans' English Classics. It contains valuable suggestions for the teacher that are pertinent to the object we have in mind here. It needs supplementing, however, by the texts of Webster's argumentative speeches. The bibliography on p. xxxiii will put the teacher in the way of many helps toward the elaboration of his course; but it calls for a few recent additions, such as Lamont's "Specimens of Exposition," Baker's "Specimens of Argumentation," Baker's "Principles of Argumentation," MacEwan's "Essentials of Argumentation," and Fack's "A Course in Argumentative Writing."

Friday afternoon "special," taking the place that used to be held by the old-fashioned Friday afternoon "rhetoricals." But such a course has so much to yield of both pleasure and profit, and has such obvious bearing upon the education for citizenship in a democracy, that we should give it an hour a week — if necessary, one of the three hours assigned to Literature — during the first or second year, or both; and in the third and fourth years would add some weeks of intensive work upon Webster and Burke, as already suggested.

In passing on now, after disposing of the whole subject of oratory and debate, to the planning of our literary studies for the second, third, and fourth years, we must not fail to note what rapid changes, what quick maturing of faculty, is taking place in our boys and girls. There is a striking difference between the first and the fourth year students; the child has become the young man and young woman — the young woman outdistancing the youth in many directions (perceptive power, artistic feelling, e.g.). and being much nearer the goal of adult ripeness. Were it not that the scale of the present treatment of our subject forbids, we should have to go into the question of the desirability of a differentiation of the work of girls and boys. Undoubtedly certain sex differences, which the teacher of English cannot fail to notice, manifest themselves at this time; and it is to our minds an open question whether regard should not be paid at this stage to these differences in the English work.[1] This rapid ripening of adult instincts and insight will make some difference in what we select, and still more in the temper in which we deal with it, the plane of our treatment.

1. The subject is touched on in Professor Clark Wissler's "The Interests of Children in the Reading Work of the Elementary School" (*Pedagogical Seminary*, Vol. V, pp. 523-540), quoted at length in Professor Thorndike's Monograph on "The Study of Children " (*Teachers College Record*, Vol. II, No. 3), which contains an allusion also (p. 29) to Miss Clara Vostrovsky's study on the same subject. See also Professor S. Thurber's address on "English Literature in Girls' Education" (*School Review*,Vol. II, 6, June, 1894). We take the opportunity to advise the young teacher to allow none of Mr. Thurber's papers, scattered through the periodicals, to escape his clutches.

As to the order of our studies, confining our attention for the moment to the works prescribed for college entrance, we may note that the lists for 1903-4-5 contain three novels and three of Shakespeare's plays. How shall we distribute these through our four years? We may reject with a mere word the proposals either to put most of them into the third and fourth years, with a view to the expediencies of examination, or to leave all the "Study" books for the fourth year. We have already disapproved of the plan to put all the novels into the first year, or even the first and second years, for the sake of parallelism with composition wok in Narration and Description respectively. We should also refuse to follow historical considerations. We must be guided by ethical and aesthetic demands. The history of literature is of secondary importance in Secondary School period. We must work with might and main for literary appreciation, regardless for the most part of all extraneous considerations. The sensible course to pursue, in dealing with Shakespeare's plays, e.g., is to deal with them in the order of their artistic and ethical complexity. "Macbeth" we shall leave to the very last, and shall have prepared the way for an appreciation of that by previous progressive work on "Julius Caesar" and "The Merchant of Venice," "As You Like It," " Midsummer Night's Dream," "Richard III," etc. Our work will have been cumulative; there will have been a gradual year-to-year growth in the power to appreciate and interpret Shakespeare.

So, too, with the three novels. The natural course to pursue will be to begin with the novel of the simplest *genre,* the historical novel and novel of adventure, — "Ivanhoe," say; then to pass on the novel of manners, the "Vicar of Wakefield," and the novel of character, "Silas Marner," so leading on, as a result of our study of George Eliot, to the more pronouncedly problem novel and psychological novel of to-day, by way of works like "Romola" and "Felix Holt," "The House of the Seven Gables," "Esmond" and "Pendennis," "Nicholas Nickleby," and ' The Tale of Two Cities " — to mention no others. This is to follow, or rather to wait upon, the maturing vision and feeling of our students. We cannot force the pace. We cannot take the kingdom of perfection by violence. We cannot despatch at a single attack this or the other type of literature. We have not a matter of scientific principle of progress to deal with here; but the gradual, insensible formation of taste, judgment, imagination, sympathy. We most heartily reecho these wise words of Professor Samuel Thurber, "If I have any pedagogic conviction more especially rooted in my philosophy than any other, it is this, — that a moral or aesthetic principle cannot be communicated *ab extra,* but must be grown up to by innumerable accretions of insight." In this spirit we say, then, in regard to the arrangement of our course of English study, that we must use our best forethought and ingenuity in planning how our students may grow up, step by step, year by year, to the appreciation in the fourth year of the "big things" on the College entrance list, and any others of our own selecting: "Macbeth," Burke on Conciliation, Milton's "Comus" and "Lycidas." Macaulay's Essay on Milton, — we do not name the "Princess," which we regard as an unwise selection, and have so learned by experience.

Guided by these general principles, we may begin our second year by working the descriptive vein. Now is the time for such works as Gray's "Elegy" (with "Thanatopsis" and Dekker's and Shirley's Verses on Death), "Childe Harold," "L'-Allegro " and "Il Penseroso," "Snowbound," "The Cotter's Saturday Night," "The Eve of St. Agnes"; for short lyrics of the more descriptive order, and a few that have the subjective touch felt in Shelley's and Wordsworth's poems on the Skylark, Emerson's "Rhodora," and Titmouse," and "Humble Bee"; while in prose we have Stevenson (the novels and "Travels with a Donkey"). "Lorna Donne" (for home reading, and class discussion), some of Burroughs's nature studies, some history selections (Green or Motley), and late in the year the " Idylls of the King" and the "Merchant of Venice" as the large items of our year's work. How these are to be utilized we shall explain in our next chapter. How to cover so much ground satisfactorily, will be explained by what we have to say concerning methods of treatment.

The third year student generally begins to show some encouraging effects of the first two years of steady work. Evidences of maturing sense of form and style, of sensitiveness to some of the finer qualities of poetry, begin to manifest themselves. This outcropping of results for which the teacher has been working patiently, are his reward for much apparently ineffectual effort during those two or three years. We can be more sturdy in our work, can attempt a little criticism and some elementary work in Æsthetics, gathering our energies for deeper appreciation in the fourth year. We may start this third year — while the principles of exposition are engaging attention in our composition— with some of Dryden and Pope. If we use that convenient collection, Syle's "From Milton to Tennyson" (Allyn & Bacon), — and we have found either that volume or Hales' "Longer English Poems" (Macmillan), or George's "Chaucer to Arnold" (Macmillan), and Pancoast's "Introduction to English Literature" (Holt) indispensable at this stage, — we shall take its appropriate selections from Dryden and Pope, adding for collateral reading "Palamon and Arcite" (for plot interest and a little comparative work with Chaucer), the "Essay on Criticism," and the "Rape of the Lock"; and then we may pass on to such recent poetry in this mode as Arnold's "Scholar Gypsy," adding "Thyrsis" and some of Arnold's lyrics, and, of course, the "Forsaken Merman," — for who would omit that bewitching, sea-sprayed song? For prose of the expository order we might take either a few of Bacon's Essays, some Bible selections, "Pilgrim's Progress," Carlyle's Essay on Burns, or Ruskin's "Sesame and Lilies." This is the year, also, for some of Lamb's Essays and Sir Roger de Coverley, perhaps some of Stevenson's Essays, and, in connection with the De Coverley papers, Macaulay's Essay on Addison. We must not forget the intensive work on Webster's orations and speeches already sketched in connection with the special course of public-speading and debating; and we must also allow time at the end to keep our progressive study of Shakespeare going, selecting "Midsummer Night's Dream," or "As You Like It," or "Twelfth Night," or one of the historical plays (We should not take at any time during the course either "Hamlet," "King Lear," or

"Othello.")

The fourth year will start with Burke's Speech on Conciliation, while the stress in our composition work is upon argument— a tough piece of work that may very well employ the fresh energies of the early part of the school year. This done, we can, with an eye both to establishing our reading in historic perspective and to refreshing our memories of works read and authors studied, go to "Macbeth" (rounding off our Shakespearean studies), then to "Comus" and "Lycidas," following it by Macaulay's Milton Essay, by means of which our students ought to have a good idea of the course of culture and literary development during the progress of the Renascence and the Reformation in England. We may then pass on to gather up the threads of that interesting "period of prose" from Dryden up through Pope, Addison, Steele, Johnson, and Goldsmith, and come to the beginning of the Romantic Movement, reserving, or reviewing "The Ancient Mariner", and grouping Byron, Keats, Wordsworth, Coleridge, and Shelley; passing on to Tennyson, with a little comparative work upon Browning, if we have a class of good enough quality to undertake the comparison. We are here suggesting the utmost that may be done with students of good quality, and in a school which avoids the make-up-for-lost-time rush of a year of cram for college.

An alternative to the historic survey and study is comparative work on the drama. Reserving "Macbeth" for the last of our studies, we can work out from in into a comparative study of some Greek tragedy (Aeschylus' "Prometheus Bound," and Sophocles' "Cedipus"), or a French or German play, according to the proficiency of our class in their French and German studies. This is a question of turning the work in other languages to account in our English class. Occasionally one may be able to utilize the Book of Job in such comparative work.

Whether we take this latter alternative will depend upon the importance we attach to a knowledge of the history of literature, and the reflection of the Zeit-Geist in the works of the masters. We should devote, we have said above, very little time in the Secondary School to historical considerations. A fair sense of historic succession may be gradually built up in the student's mind. Each new author read should be put into time-relations with those already studied, and occasionally the cultural evolution of the period may be touched upon. We know no more effective way of doing this than to work out with increasing detail a chart in which should be incorporated the salient historic facts as they emerge. Nicols's and Ryland's Tables of Literature and History will be useful in this connection and so will the tables in Pancoast's History and in Longmans' or other editions of School Classics.

Just how far the personal and biographical interest — the time and place interest, the anecdotal interest — shall be developed in our work, it is impossible to say with any touch of dogmatism. The teacher's leading purpose must be to get the student to read, appreciate, and evaluate the great creative works. He will grudge much time taken from that to read books about books. He may flavor at times with the solider kind of literary gossip. When he is reading Goldsmith and Johnson with his class, it would be strange were he not tempted into the by-paths of picturesque personalities by Boswell's "Johnson," which he should consider it wicked not to introduce to his students. Much may be introduced by the way. Occasional lantern talks and lectures on general topics should be given; and generous but judicious use made of pictures of authors and places, and illustrated editions of their works (Abbey's "Shakespeare," Thompson's "Sir Roger," etc.) The students may use illustrative material in their note-books, and contribute to a general school collection. The more suggestive and speaking the class-room atmosphere, the better. Few of us will be able to realize what Mr. George has realized in his English room at Newton, but we can all strive for something of the sort; we can all keep advancing toward the goal set up by Professor Genung in the following stimulating passage:-

"Our school rooms suggest in various ways the matter-of-fact, the practical, the utilitarian, and this is right, benches and desks are for study; books to be thumbed and ground up into lessons; inkstands and pads for fingers, formula, notes. All this is emphatically the prose of school life. Now I would have the class room, if I could, decorated with such pictures, books, busts, and the like, as would help the room in some degree to support the taste for refinement and beauty, history and imagination. I would have the faces of great poets and thinkers looking down upon the student's work. I would have some good books there; such especially as would not only be of practical value, but would give the student an idea of a good edition and a worthy form of publication. I would have some of the great scenes of history and poetry shining before him in works of art; so that entering here he might come out of the sordid, everyday surroundings into a region sacred to higher things. There is too little of this in our schools; too little of the spiritual and high-minded. And there is perhaps no class room so well calculated to foster this as the class room wherein we think and talk of great writers and their art."[1]

1 "The Teacher's Outfit in Rhetoric, " *School Review*, Vol. III, No. 7, September, 1895.

2

Literature in the Secondary School: Methods of Study

THE fact that such works as "The Ancient Mariner," "The Vision of Sir Launfal," "Ivanhoe," "The Last of the Mohicans," which are commonly read in the "Elementary School, are among those prescribed for the College entrance examinations, indicates that no hard-and-fast line can be drawn between works especially suitable for either the Elementary School or the Secondary School. As we have said before, some works are universal in their appeal, and speak to the children of all ages. They mean much or little, according to the range of the heart and mind to which they appeal. This fact indicates the only safe point of view from which to approach the problems of method in the Secondary School. A teacher soon discovers that the treatment of "The Ancient Mariner" in the first year of the Secondary School cannot be what it should be in the fourth year, when the student knows more, and is so much riper in judgment and feeling. Hence there are pitfalls in outlining methods applicable to the Secondary school period. Some teachers are misled by elaborate, overedited editions of the prescribed classics into inflexible methods. Regardless of widely varying conditions, they pay unaltering regard to the same minutiae of editorial scholarship; and so they are lost in details, and slight the large, life-giving features of their work. But the rule of the text-books is impossible, if only because they set such different standards. We could name recent text-books that, by their method of presentation and editorial profusion, are unsuited to any but good fourth year or postgraduate classes; others that are not up to the level of average first-year classes. There must be discrimination here, based on a recognition of the great differences that, in the four years of adolescent growth, distinguish the graduate from the freshman. There are as many ways of dealing with a book as there are phases in human development.

Trying to find a foothold to stay ourselves in our quest for methods adapted to these varying circumstances of the High School period, we may start from these two facts: it is in this period that the average student (there are exceptions) develops a pronounced interest in poetry, feels deeply for the first time the emotional appeal of poetry; and for the first time manifests a keen appreciation of style and an increasing responsiveness to beauty. (Girls are ahead of boys in this respect.) This is what we might deduce from the characteristics of adolescence. The tense, surging emotionalism of youth engenders a new and respectful feeling for the celestial madness of the poet. Hyperbole comes natural at this time. No language is too extravagant for the spellbound, ebullient maid and youth. The tropes of a Romeo and a Juliet, who are the fascinating classic types of adolescent perfervidness in speech, are after his manner. And with this acceptance of highly emotionalized speech comes the feeling for style, — the sensuous element in literature, — the ebb and flow of rhythm, the picturesqueness of figure, the heightened colour of words.

These emotional developments give us our unique opportunities in the Secondary School. Clearly, to be putting over philological microscopy, or hedging our students about with dictionaries enyclopeadias, etc., when we can be feeding and developing ethical and aesthetic insight and appreciation, is a fatal mistake. Here is a chance to establish a life-long delight in literary excellence and in communion with the great spirits of the past. To succeed in that must be our master-aim; so that methods must first of all look toward the larger ethical and aesthetic values in literary study. We may now enlist the waxing passion for beauty in behalf of ultimate ethical aims; find new approaches to the true and the good by the avenue of the beautiful. This means that in the study of poetry we must be careful not to damage its essentially poetical quality in our eagerness to rationalize it, to clear up difficulties of secondary importance, to master the minutiae of allusion and diction. We can afford to emphasize the stylistic element. For example, — to speak of our study of prose,— we shall do well to select chiefly writers whose distinctive qualities of style give interesting individuality to their work; those who, like Macaulay and De Quincey, Stevenson and Lowell, and the masters of impassioned and imaginative oratory like Webster, have obvious and at times exaggerated stylistic traits, rather than those who, although sager as models, — Addison and Goldsmith, Irving, Cooper and Thackeray, — have less striking peculiarities.[1]

In this connection we must emphasize the increasing rather than the waning importance of reading aloud as the best means of bringing out the expressiveness of poetry and prose. Whereas, before this time, it has been chiefly the straight forward singsong of verse and the simpler forms of stanza that have been appreciated, now we note the rapid growth of a power to enjoy the subtler beauties: the variations and irregularities of Shakespeare's, Milton's, and Tennyson's blank verse; the ripe metric art revealed so clearly in "Macbeth"; the involved, climactic phrasings of the Spenserian stanza and the sonnet. It is in close connection with this oral interpretation of masterpieces that we would take up the principles of versification, holding firmly to the point of view that an analysis of verse forms and the scansion of lines are to be purely in the interest of sympathetic and ex-

1. The trend of opinion has been steadily in this direction of working for the large ethical and esthetic values. Compare, e.g., those early Clarendon Press editions of Shakespeare, to which we were many of us so deeply indebted, which deliberately eschew literary or aesthetic annotations, with the most recent American school editions of the plays, say, Professor Katherine Lee Bates's edition of "A Midsummer Night's Dream" (Leach, Shewell, and Sanborn), the notes of which, divided into Textual, Grammatical, and Literary, give sixty-three pages to the last named and twenty-seven pages to the other two combined.

pressive oral rendering. Our scansion must be a scheme of notation indicative of the accent and emphasis, tone and tempo, to be accorded in reading. We shall indicate more definitely what we mean in outlining presently a graded course in versification.[1]

And now for the application of these and other related principles. The first year is a year of beginnings, and therefore of cautious and somewhat tentative work. Our plan, with some filling out in connection with the course in composition, will be this: we shall get under way with some short stories, varying in character; pass on to the ballad (the short story in verse) and epic type; then (ringing again the changes upon the differences between prose forms and verse forms) take up the novel; and conclude with a play, with its last lessons for the year on the structure of the "tale that is told." in its several varieties of form.

We have often used Hawthorne's "Twice-told Tales" to begin with, because, certain drawbacks notwithstanding, they include conveniently in one volume many well-nigh perfect types of story and sketch, which our students may distinguish, classify, and compare: the monologue-like "Rill from the Town Pump" and the plotless "Toll-gatherer's Day"; the simple incident type, "David Swan," and the more dramatic "Gray Champion "; that masterful study in incident, character, and suggestive meaning, "The Ambitious Guest"; the dramatic allegory, "Dr. Heidegger's Experiment"; the sequence of quasi-historic sketches, "Legends of the Province House," so full of atmosphere and interwoven ethical intention. Another advantage which these stories possess is that some of them reveal the actual process of the writer's creative art; we see, e.g., out of what original materials of fact, and what added, intensifying material of imagination, the "Ambitious Guest" and the "Great Carbuncle" were magically elaborated. In this connection it is easy to interest the student in Hawthorne himself, his personality and his shy, retired, shadow-haunted life, as he is reflected in some of the stories, and as he

1. We may now add Stevenson to those who illustrate the importance of the oral element in developing style. Says his recent biographer, "In his own delicate hearing lay perhaps the root of his devotion to style." Balfour's "Life," Vol. II, p. 193.

discloses himself in his Preface; and if a study of the "House of the Seven Gables" is to follow in the second or third years, this will be valuable as preparation and foreground. Also, topical reports may be made upon assigned portions of the Preface to the "Scarlet Letter," upon Hawthorne's "Life and Letters," and sundry magazine articles, especially those on "A Glimpse into Hawthorne's Workshop," and "Hawthorne's Salem," published years ago in the *Century.* It will be well to supplement this exclusively Hawthorne work by a study of two or three short stories of quite different temper and kind, — such, let us say, as Mr. Quililer-Couch's "Roll Call of the Reef," Mr. Davis's Van Bibber Stories, or some of Mr. Kipling's best work, — indeed, there is a wide range of choice from Poe, Harte, Stockton, Howells, Bunner, Hamlin Garland, Miss Jewett, Miss Wilkins, etc.

This work should be simply and quickly and, above all, cleanly done, without dissipating the characteristic atmosphere and suggestiveness of the stories — things that must be *felt,* and recognized, either overtly or tacitly. The main matter in this story work, however, is structure, the anatomy and logic of form in its most obvious aspects, consisting chiefly in a clear perception of what gives unity to each story, of the relation of the parts (episode and incident) to the whole; and of the ways in which effects of expectation and premonition, delay and surprise, climax and catastrophe, are produced. The stories may be assigned sometimes singly (one preparation and recitation will suffice for the shortest) and sometimes in pairs for comparative purposes. Having been neatly disposed of, they should leave a helpful residuum of notes, outlines, graphic diagrams, summaries, and reports, and, in connection with the composition work, compositions, reductions, imitations, etc. all of which should prove useful for reference purposes later on.

And here we may interpose what we have to say about note-taking. It is very easy to overdo this business; and yet we are not of those who would dispense with notes altogether. The note-book must never be a substitute or maid-in-waiting for the memory, or an aid to cramming: inveterate note-takers injure both memory and the power of intense, sustained attention. It must not be a collection of essays or even of sentences, nor a carry-all of unassorted, unorganized scraps and siftings caught from the teacher's table. It should not wastefully reproduce anything that is in books used of easily accessible. It should be, no less than is a science note-book, a graphic, shorthand presentation of solution of literary problems, — parallelisms, comparisons, etc. We should lay it down as a general rule, that no notes are to be made for the sake of mere recall, but for the sake of the powers called into play in making them. In their simplest form they should involve some selecting and organizing of data. These data should be organized in such a way as to tell their story by their very appearance, — clear heading and subheadings, and well-articulated outlines, — and, be it added, by the absence of fussy and futile rulings and flourishes and beribbonings. The report of a lecture heard should take this outline form, a care for the thought being uppermost, and the thought-relations to be indicated by the form. These expressive outlines, tables, charts, diagrams, maps, and other ingenuities of condensation should be the bulk of the matter in the note-book; and it should give indications that the individuality of the student has been worked into it. Approximative models or suggestions may be given by the teacher for the various kinds of notes, as the students are called upon to make them. The notes should be inspected from time to time, and appraised chiefly on the score of their convenient brevity and formal expressiveness; it being the object of the teacher in his corrections and deletions to educate the student's perception of relative values, teaching him to strain away from the salient and focal facts of a subject all the merely savorless and marginal facts.

We must not overlook, however, the value of the mere writing up of rough notes as compelling the student to recall and rethink the living commentary and discussion of the class. That is why we would not prohibit altogether notes on words, idioms, etc., in the works studied. The more or less mechanical work of expanding the hurried jotting or symbol of the moment into a significant note which the student thinks it worth while, for future serviceableness, to put down, may be made a part of the process of assimilation through reflection. We have found it convenient — in the study of Shakespeare and Milton especially — to get students to classify the most significant words in this wise:-

Notes on Diction

Obsolete	*Changed in Meaning of Usage*	*Differently pronounced*	*Idioms, etc.*
"Merchant of	Venice."		
28 Vailing - bowing	17 still-always	8 o-ce-a	144 Childhood(s) proof
110 Gear-purpose	175 thrift-success, cf. "thrifty."	54 as-pect	185 of my trust
161 Prest-ready cf. Fr. pret. -prest.			
	61 prevented-come before. Cf. Bible use.		
"L'Allegro."			
12yclept:-called cf. German "get-" in past. part.	67 tells his tale { - counts : cf. "teller" in a bank - total, cf. "tally" and "talesman."	138 pierce - like "verse" (still so in N. E. family name).	33 trip it, cf. "go it" and "stop it."

In the case of Gray's "Elegy" the student may be asked what words or phrases remind him of Milton (if he has read the shorter poems); or in Goldsmith's poems what words recall the usage of earlier poets, or have changed their meaning in any way since Goldsmith's time.

Studies plot are tabulated and diagrammed, — e.g., the plot of "Silas Marner " in double columned table showing the interplay of "Marner" and "Cass" threads; that of the 'Merchant of Venice" and "As You Like It" in five columns showing to excellent purpose the more complex web of those plots; while the plot of 'Macbeth" may be diagrammed after the pyramidal manner adopted by Freytag in his "Technique of the Drama," and followed, after Freytag's pattern, by Miss Woodward in her volume on the drama.

So, too, character-groups, pairs, contrasts, foils, are graphically presented in intersection circles, enchainments, etc., according to the students' preferences and ingenuities. Places associated with authors or works, and journeys like Quentin Durward's, or Milton's or Goldsmith's travels, may be located on outline maps. All such devices, we repeat, should be designed to throw upon the pupil tasks of selecting and organizing his material with scientific purpose. Special attention should be paid to note-taking and note-making in the first year of Secondary School work.

After this necessary digression we may resume the consideration of our main topic, the treatment of the works selected for the first year.

We are now to pass, in our first year's work, from the short story to the epic or narrative poem; but not, let us note, without some work of a descriptive, expository, and critical nature in connection with the study of Hawthorne's life and personality. In this biographical work our principle of progressive development from year to year may be followed; and in it, too, the point to be kept to the fore, in the selection of data is the relative value of the facts. We shall ask: What events are important in Hawthorne's — Milton's — Gray's — Goldsmith's — life ? Why ? One biographical formula, we must point out, will not do for all types of life and character: the influences of parentage and place, of nature and books, of society and solitude, of health or sickness, of early education or its neglect, of romance or routine, of ease or hardship, — these influences may count for much or for little; and we must help our students to seize and interpret those dominant characteristics of a person and his career which reflect themselves in the works we examine.

In dealing now with the epic or narrative poem — be it one of Scott's or the Phaeacian episodes from the "Odyssey," or Arnold's "Sohrab and Rustum" or "Balder Dead" — we shall drive home in new ways the principles of construction studied in the short story; and we shall try to bring out the differences between prose and poetry as vehicles. Here are a few leading questions : What can the poet do, as story-teller and plot-maker, that the prose writer does not and cannot do ? and why? For instance, what liberties may the poet take in the way of descriptive amplifications and digressions? What magic of musical witchery does he employ to check the flow if his story and to detach our interest for a time from the main matter ? Why can he impose upon us these catalogues of names, these repetition, these little asides, these long-drawn similes, these comeos of irrelevant description ? Why are we so ready to lend an ear to his — "Ah ! that reminds me" ? How much is Scott or Homer, Arnold or Morris (if we glance at his "Jason" or "Atlanta's Race") or Tennyson given to these things ? Let us see what, in Scott's "Marmion" or "Lady of the Lake," is of capital plot interest, and what is of subordinate, episodic interest ? Where are we delayed ? Let us take stock of the nature of these delays — show them in a table or diagram. Where are there musical interludes, as in an opera? Are they worth while? Do they justify themselves?

This is the direction we should take, and how far we shall go in this direction must depend upon circumstances. Can we do anything better than work along these lines to enable the student to get a grip at once on the plot, on character and scenic interest, and on the style of the work ? We believe not. These things hang together; they give meaning to one another; they illustrate the prime principles of unity and variety in unity, and the meaning and the limited application of the canon of Aesthetic, — that beauty is its own excuse for being, — as nothing else can.

Following these lines, we may consider wherein our treatment of Scott's "Lay of the Last Minstrel: would differ from that we have suggested in Chapter 10 for the higher Grammar Grades. We shall work in a larger way. After the first rapid reading in the manner therein indicated, — the vocal rendering of the finer parts by the teacher being the leading feature, — we shall diagram or outline the plot in such a way as to show the firm, clear course of the main story, and the branching of the subordinate episodes, digressions, asides, etc. These we shall discuss. Would we omit or skip any of them ? Does this or that one seem to be mere padding, or a freakish indulgence of poetic high spirits ? The dull and unappreciative will be for omitting; the more susceptible will insist that this seeming digression is necessary for the light it sheds on the circumstances of the action or on a character, or is a small but indispensable link in the chain of events. This real digression, idyllic or lyric or reflective, is justified by the fact that it restfully lowers the pitch of excitement for a moment, or prepares us the better for the stress that is to follow; while this other we would not dispense with because it is so fine, — "Why, those two lines make it worth while !" And so considerations of structure will lead us on to considerations of style, and exhibit the common-sense logic of style.

This reading of one of Scott's poems might be preceded or followed by a reading of Arnold's "Sohrab and Rustum," — for the sake of its Homeric qualities, its close-knit structure, the splendid crescendo from the hush and first stirrings of the dawn up to the moment when "the noise of battle hurtles in the air;" and the diminuendo down to that last scene of silence and of night. The presence and the significance of Homeric simile, epithet, refrain-like repetitions and enumerations, might be brought out by a little comparative work with a selection from Homer. In fact, we should lose no chance to work by comparison: the Secondary School freshman is ready for more advanced work in this direction. For instance, in the study of Bryant's version of the parts of the "Odyssey" before alluded to ("Ulysses among the Phaeacians"), we ourselves have found that a comparison of Bryant with Pope, Butcher and Lang, Palmer, and Mackail has helped often to sharpen the appreciation of style in surprising manner. We may add that we like to find an opportunity thus early in the course for a good example of blank verse, to serve as a beginning of our studies and exercises in verification.

Concerning the study of novel, to follow this work with the narrative poem, not much need be said. The work may be less schematic and detailed than what we have been doing so far. It will be a change to work from the character side of plot, and to mine the character interest. A few general questions on the plot (Where is the climax ? What are the factors in the entanglement? Where is the movement of the story most rapid? Where slowest?) may be followed by character analysis of the hero, heroine, and villain; and then by questions on the style (What is the best description of (a) scene ? (b) a person in outward presentment ? (c) a character ? How much dialogue is there ? When does it come ? Does it advance the plot ? Has the prose any notable qualities of rhythm ? of imagery ?), to which we may add any questions as to paragraph or sentence characteristics that may hitch with our composition work.

And now we may quiet down to a short spell of work on the author, Scott, — if it is one of his novels we have been reading. We may read parts of Irving's Essay (the account of his visit to Abbotsford) and some good critical essay (say, Andrew Lang's in his volume of 'Essays in Little," which conveniently contains an essay on Dumas). We may work out some preferences — Scott, Henty, Cooper, Dumas, Kingsley — according to the reading of the class.

Finally, we shall reach Shakespeare, — "Julius Caesar," — if it has not already been read. Let the teacher read it through, with a minimum of comment, to the class; and it will pay to have spared no pains to become proficient in this task. Professor Corson, in his little book on "The Voice and Spiritual Education" (which with the companion volume on "The Aims of Literary Study" should receive every teacher's careful attention and study), quotes Sir Henry Taylor as saying that he regarded the reading of Shakespeare to boys and girls, if he be well read and they are apt, "as carrying with it a deeper cultivation than anything else which can be done to cultivate them." Experience has proved to us that there is scarcely any exaggeration in these words. There are few gifts, if any, that will atone for the absence in an English teacher, of the powers to read Shakespeare well, — we do not mean read him as platform readers do, with great pomp and ceremony; but clearly, with pleasant tone, and good enunciation, and with the feeling, the sincerity, the earnestness, and the artistic conscience that are born of the desire to awaken in young hearers a love of the master. We recall a Secondary School teacher whose pupils, after going in a class to a Christmas reading of the "Christmas Carol" by a justly famous reader, declared that they much preferred their own instructor's way; the moral of which is, we think, that the teacher is able, in the close intimacy and freedom of the class room, to grip the heart and understanding of his class as no platform-artist possibly can.

This first reading of "Julius Caesar" by the teacher should have left upon his students a deep and lasting impression of the play in its totality, with the parts in due perspective, of its essentially dramatic and rhythmic features (its rise and fall of emotional emphasis), and of its poetic power. This will provide a basis for the development work that is to follow. First, we shall call for an outline or synopsis of the scenes to reveal the plot. This must be done with utmost brevity in terms of what happens, of action. So we shall develop insight into the first essential of dramatic art: that it is concerned with what men *do* under the stress of temptation, struggle, opportunity. And so we may bring out the differentiae of the drama as compared with the epic, the novel, the short story.

Our second reading, by the class, calling for the memorizing and presentation of selected scenes by the students, will be an exercise in interpretation, and will involve the clearing up of such difficulties in metrics, in words, constructions, and allusions, as stand in the way of such oral rendering and interpretation. This should be our practical test: Do we understand? The teacher may introduce the subject by explaining to the class that the language of Shakespeare's time, while (as they will have noticed) very much like our own, yet had its peculiarities, which sometimes stand in our way (obsolete words and idioms) and sometimes mislead us (changes in meaning and pronunciation). This is obvious in the opening of the first scene. The class may point out the words, — " mechanical,." "ought not walk," "laboring day," "profession," "cobbles" (for the pun), "naughty " "knave,"vulgar," etc., — an excellent crop ! Well, we must be sure, as we go, that we are not being tripped up in our attempt to decipher what Shakespeare means. The teacher will not press the matter far, but will let the niceties alone. The feeling for Shakespearean English must grow gradually from year to year. The students may tabulate in their note-book (see Table on p. 28) twenty salient examples culled from the text. When this second circumspect, interpretative reading is done, we may review the ground covered, and round off our studies in language by working out a few parallelisms (of the teacher's selection) between Shakespeare's English and Bible English — a first step toward a literary study of the Bible (this also in tabular form).

The talk on the metrics — with perhaps a short exercise or two — may come when the first difficulties occur, as they will in the first and second scenes: as e.g., the transition from the prose of the "base mechanicals" to the verse of the dignified tribunes, the short lines, the free movement of the verse, the differences of pronunciation (touched, spirit, construe), the presence of rhyme, etc. The motive of such work, we repeat, must be the desire to deliver the lines effectively. One good exercise to test appreciation of rhythm is to require students to divide into lines passages written on the board in lineless prose form. At this point, too, we may test familiarity with the play by short class exercises, asking by whom certain important lines were spoken.

Now the way is clear for character-study, leading on into the deeper study of the plot, with which it is to some extent involved. This may be by means of problems, or in question form. For example, we may ask: "What mistakes did Brutus make ? And what light do they throw upon his character ?" Or we may call for a tabular presentation of Caesar's character (data for a composition) thus:-

Qualities of Character	*Evidence*			
	Act	*Scene*	*Line*	*Words or Incident cited*

Or we may ask for a comparative study, in similar form, of Calpurnia and Portia, or a contrast between Brutus and Caesar.

Lastly, returning to plot again, we may try to master its logic. Here are some of the questions we may put (sometimes the class is equal to only one or two of the simpler of them):-

1. Seeing that Caesar is killed so early in the play, how is the title to be justified ? Is he the hero ?
2. Does Caesar's death mark the climax ? If so, how is the interest sustained in the major portion of the play which follows ?
3. Why is Scene I a good opening scene ? Of what facts and circumstances does it put us in possession ? In what state of mind does it leave us ?
4. Could we omit the scene with Cinna the poet ?
5. What object is served by the scene between Portia, Lucius, and the Soothsayer ?
6. Why the scene introducing Cicero, who appears this once only ?
7. Why does the Ghost appear to Brutus rather than to Cassius ?

Or, if our class is equal to it, we can enumerate (in table) Shakespeare's departures from Plutarch, and try to discover the reason for them.

We have left untouched any discussion of the ethics of the play, and the rhetorical exercises that may grow out of it. These will be incidental for the most part. Such questions as — Was Caesar's assassination justifiable ? Why do we condemn Brutus's suicide ? — are sure to arise. Sometimes these problems can be turned over to the debating class. It is in connection also with the work in public speaking and argument that we would deal with the speeches of Brutus and Antony — a comparison of the prose style of the one (why prose ?) with the verse style of the other; and an analysis of the parts in their effect upon the audience. While the many opportunities the play presents for work in Narration, Description, and Exposition will be utilized in connection with the course in Composition, we must use these exercises to help the imaginative grasp of the circumstances and setting of the play. What sort of man was Caesar to outward view, as Shakespeare presents him ? — is an instance. Or we have given as a general topic "A Streets Scene in Rome, : asking each student to describe as he sees it, vividly in his mental eye, any one street scene in which the populace of Rome share, -- that mob whose presence is felt, whose murmur is heard, so continually throughout the play. Various moments of the play will be selected.

We have still to consider how we shall provide for a study of the life and times of Shakespeare, and of the matters connected therewith. We have generally found time for a mastering of the few facts about his life in the first year. In the second year we have placed in our pupils' hands Dowden's "Primer"; and in the third and fourth years have sent them for amplifications to Lee's Life, Dowden's larger work, "Shakespeare, his Mind and Art," Moulton's Shakespeare as a Dramatic Artist"; and have put them in touch, for special purposes, with Hudson's "Shakespeare's Life, Art and Character," Ward's "English Dramatic Literature, " Coleridge's "Lectures on Shakespeare, "Halliwell-Phillips' "Outlines of the Life of Shakespeare," and Furness's Varircum Edition of the plays.[1] We have found it convenient to distribute the topics of this supplementary work thus :-

1. Valuable suggestions to teachers for the advanced studies which it is essential for them to undertake, will be found in the pamphlet, "English is Secondary Schools, " by Professors Gayley and Bradley of the University of California (published by the University, at Berkeley).

Ist year, Life of Shakespeare.

2nd year, The Age of Shakespeare, with special reference to the theatre.

3rd year, Periods of his dramatic activity: facts as to folios, quartos, etc.

4th year, His dramatic development: internal evidences chiefly.

In this chapter our outline of the first year's work has been interrupted by a necessary treatment of such topics as note-taking, Shakespearean studies, etc. These we have thought it better to treat incidentally as they arose than to defer for separate treatment elsewhere.

At this pausing point we may remark upon the impossibility of dealing, in a treatise so general in scope as this one, with the manifold problems of Secondary School work. We shall hope to have covered the leading problems; but even this necessitates an exposition so condensed and rapid as to court some danger of confusion.

What we have said about the leading features of the work of the first year renders unnecessary an equally detailed treatment of the work of the three following years. At the beginning of the second year the emphasis shifts from the narrative — that is, preeminently the structural aspect of literary art — to the descriptive — that is, preeminently its colour and music, its impressionistic aspect. Wholes are now of less importance: parts of more. We shall aim to get our pupils to see and feel now how a perfectly simple idea can clothe itself or unfold itself in a fascination manner by means of image, association, and enriched musical language. Milton's "L'Allegro" and "Il Penserosoe," Gray's "Elegy," and Goldsmith's "Deserted Village" are all excellent for this purpose, and all of them interest students at this time. Milton is especially good because his pair of poems allow of comparative work, and give us at the same time the beginning of three years' progressive work on Milton. It is partly for these reasons, but even more because of the varied and telling work that may be done with them, that we use them to exemplify our treatment of this type of poem.

First, of all, vocal rendering becomes increasingly important; for the beauties of these poems can be revealed to the full only through the lips. Milton's extreme sensitiveness to vocal effectiveness is evident in them in many ways. There is nothing better to be found to illustrate the expressive values of changes in rhythm, accent, and quantity, changes in time and tone, changes from crisp staccato to smooth legato effects.

The poems having been read by the teacher, with enough explanation and discussion to bring into relief the mood that dominates each, and the means by which the contrasting ideas and tempers are bodied fourth (the day-time social blitheness of the cheerful man, and the night-time solitary joyousness of the meditative man), the class may at once be set to memorizing and rendering the limes while the cadences are fresh upon the ear. With this will go discussion and elucidation of the metrics and a few metrical exercises, while the detailed parallelisms and contrasts will be brought out. In the former we shall do justice, (1) to the lovely change from the harsh and trailing lines of the introductory dismissal, to the light and flowing lines of the invitation to the 'godesse fair and free," or, in' "Il Penseroso." to the richer, graver, fluted tones of the address to the "godesse sage and holy"; (2) to the frequent changes in the lines from the iambic to the trochaic accent (to put the matter in ordinary terms); (3) to the exquisite modulation of the tempo (noticeably through the differences in vowel values), as when, in the midst of caprice-like daintiness of the—

"Come, and trip it, as you go,
On the light fantastic toe,"

we have the *rallentando*, the slower, fuller-vowelled, monosyllabic movement, the firmer tread, the check of a touch of the poet's reserved seriousness, with—

"And in thy right hand lead with thee
The mountain nymph, sweet Liberty,"

a slight but very significant out-cropping of the poet's spiritual passion, which the student will later appreciate when he follows the steady, heroic march of the master toward that goal of freedom which is registered in the series of poems that closes with "Lycidas."

The parallelisms and contrasts may conveniently be registered in some such manner as this:-

Lines	*"L'Allegro"*	*Lines*	*"IL Penseroso"*
1-10	Dismissal, —of Melancholy.	1-10	of deluding joys.
11-46	Invitation of Mirth.	11-54	to Melancholy.
47-150	Progress of day of social delights.	55-174	of night of solitary joys.
42	(*a*) Lark's Reveille—	56	(*a*) Evening.
44	(*b*) "Dappled Dawn," cock, hounds, etc.	67	(*b*) Nightingale's even-song.
60	(*c*) Sunrise.	74	(*c*) Moonrise.
	(*d*) Sounds of labor.		(*d*) Curfew.
	(It will be well to quote the lines.)		
Or we may include such details as the following :—			
	Descent of Mirth: —		of Melancholy :
	Venus and Bacchus: Youth and Jollity; or		Vesta and Saturn; that is, Domestic Quiet and Solitariness.
	Milton's own=Zephyr and Aurora : the light some west-wind and the spirit of morning		
	Mirth=a nymph.		Melancholy=a nun.
	Her companions : etc., etc.		Her companions :

Then we may deal more thoroughly with the descriptive features of the verse, — in pause, word, phrase, figure, and imagery; in alliterative and onomatopoetic effects; in mental picture and sensuous musical quality.

Afterward, we may reach behind the poems to the poet: What kind of personality is it that expresses itself thus in two such moods ? Is it a rich, large one ? a nature-loving one ? book-loving ? music-loving ? theatre-haunting ? By what is it attracted in nature ? By sights or sounds or odors ? by color or motion ? near or distant landscape ? Are there evidences of fine observation ? Think of some other poet's way of looking at Nature. What are his intellectual interests ? His favourite authors ? And this may lead to looking up and capturing the facts as to Milton's early life up to the Horton period.

The opportunities for descriptive composition in connection with the poem are as many as the teacher is inclined to utilize.

As to what should follow this work on Milton, we shall be guided by the outcome of what we have done, and the state of mind in which we find the class. Sometimes it is desirable to catch a deeply-aroused interest in this type of literature by passing on at once to the "Deserted Village," or Gray's "Elegy"; or (striking a contrast between the Miltonic and the modern romantic) to pass to Byron's "Childe Harold" or Keats's "Eve of St. Agnes," — which has the attractiveness of a narrative interest along with its tapestried richness of descriptive beauty. Or it may be the nature-side of the poems that has kindled interest; and we may catch this wave, and also make a desirable change to prose by taking an essay or two by Burroughs or another, or some of the nature poems in Syle's volume . Or we may take up Stevenson on the descriptive side, with "Travels with a Donkey" or "An Inland Voyage" for text, and a plentiful supplement of descriptive matter drawn from his essays and sketches. The state of the work in Composition will, of course, be a factor in our choice. That may have revealed a special weakness in observation, or what not, which it may be well to strengthen by intensive study of those authors who are especially strong in this quality.

These ends, along with others may indeed be pursued by turning at once to fiction, — to "Silas Marner" or "Lorna Doone," both strong in descriptive power. The scene at the Rainbow in the former will be a pendant to the cottage tale-telling scene in "L'Allegro," and will help us in an inventive effort to elaborate that scene, and present the credulous peasantry of the seventeenth century. "Lorna Doone" transports us back almost to the very period, and its profuse description will give us copious material for analytical and imitative work.

Of these two works, "Silas Marner" will afford us the better opportunity to carry forward our studies of fictitious narrative. Novel reading is such a large factor in our modern life and culture, that it is worth while to help our students to adopt proper standards and cultivate a sound taste in their choice of fiction. "Silas Marner: forms an excellent bridge from the Scott type of the fiction of adventure to the modern novel of character problems and of sociological import. Let it be read at home, and reviewed in some rapid way in the class. We have found the plan of requiring the class to invent good titles to the chapters effective; this exercise provokes profitable discussion of the question as to what are the salient points of the story. Then the plot may be diagrammed as suggested on page 282 and the central, unifying idea of the story brought out. It will be well then, with the plot diagram before us, to go over the book chapter by chapter, scrutinizing more carefully the part each plays in relation to the main idea. A good many interesting questions may be put in this connection, e.g., :-

What periods of time elapse in the story ? Give references.

What object is served by introducing Sally Oates in Chapter II ?

What is Dolly Winthrop's part in the development of the plot ?

Would the story suffer by cutting out the confab at the Rainbow?[1] etc

The problems of character will follow; and the more trenchantly they are put, the better. For example, we may ask, concerning Miss Nancy: Would she, in our estimate of her, have refused Godfrey Cass if she had known of his first marriage? There will remain such questions as to language and style, time and place interest, the author and her works, the dominant ethical problems of the play, — fate and character, retribution and expiation, — as are in order according to the plane of the class in intelligence and cultivation. The class may be asked to cull four or five of the profoundest reflections on the graver problems of life. With girls , at least, it is easy to arouse a deep interest in the personality and literary career of George Eliot.

We have still, according to our plan, the "Idylls of the King" and the "Merchant of Venice" to provide for . We may interpose, if time allows, something of the essay kind, — Lamb or Bacon, Ruskin or Carlyle (a chapter from "Heroes"). We have sometimes read, in order to play into the hands of the composition work, Poe's essay on the Poetic Principle; and have developed the aesthetics of literary description as compared with the descriptive powers of the space arts. This work, however, had better be considered in connection with the course in Composition and Rhetoric.

Of the treatment of the "Idylls " and the "Merchant," little need there be said: it will follow the lines laid down for the first year work with the narrative poem and with "Julius Caesar." Tennyson's epic will give us a rare chance to follow out our distinctions between prose and poetry by using Malory's prose version for comparative purposes; it will introduce us to a more complex and ornate form of blank verse; above all it will give food for thought and investigation by reason of the separate problems or ideas that are worked out in each self-

1. Teachers will receive valuable help in pressing this side of their work from the notes to Professor Jones's edition of "Silas Marner" (Appleton).

sufficient section of the poem, and the great underlying problem of the whole both its direct and its symbolic meaning. But the main thing is close, sympathetic contact with Arthurian romance, with its high, chivalrous ideals, and its by-paths up into those high altitudes of Celtic legend and heroism of which mention has already been made. Mere contact with this world is a great education; and Tennyson gives it such rich emblazonry, and presents its heroic figures with such noble gait, that it ought to contribute a deep and lasting element to the spiritual enlargement of our students . It will be well to draw upon other poets to supplement Tennyson here and there, — an Arthurian poem or two by Morris, or Arnold's "Tristram and Iseult."

In the third year we exploit new vein, in connection with the attempt to conquer the principles and art of exposition. We pass from the romantic to the classic mode; from the masters of imagination and inspired spontaneity, to the masters of a more deliberative and calculation temper. Our programme, we may recall (see page 266) is to begin with Dryden and Pope, and to pass on to the study of Addison's and Steele's prose as the ripe fruit of the new tendency toward an easier, more lucid, and more measured prose style. From the expository manner — equable, unagitated — we may proceed to expository method; then — because it will follow naturally upon our reading in the "Spectator" — we may take Macaulay's "Essay on Addison," a fairly good example of the biographical order, which will give us work in structural analysis that will be valuable.

Without being slavishly governed by the needs of our expository work in Composition, we may indirectly and directly contribute to that work. To live in the atmosphere of the period from 1650-1750, — the Age of Reason, Common Sense, Prose,— will, in itself, be helpful. We shall be studying the new critical and self-conscious spirit which owed mush to French influence, in the Epistles of Dryden and pope (the "Essay on Criticism" or "Essay on Man"); in some of the "Spectator" papers- e.g., on Party Politics," "The Over crowding of the Learned Professions," "On Country Manners" ; and, if we revert to an earlier type for the sake of comparison, one or two of Bacon's Essays. Here will be plenty of opportunity to study how an idea or given line of thought may be worked out, and to realizing that, whereas in narration and description there are conditions and props to guide us (sequence in time, relations in space, etc.), in the expository type of writing we must rely solely on the logic of thought-connection, — on definition, proportion, restraint. Here is a craftsmanship that is governed by cautious, ingenious planning, and calls for clearness in procedure and expression,—a Popean neatness and appositeness, an Addisonian limpidity and ease. Such are the virtues we shall strive to discover and appreciate, and to embody in turn in our own attempts.

But this aim is not to deflect us from our chief concern,—that of getting our students to understand and enjoy each work according to its proper and peculiar excellences, the compact sententiousness and trenchant aphoristic quality of Dryden's and Pope's epistles; the fine-mannered, delightful characterization of the "Spectator" papers, their vivid recall of the London and the rural England of good Sir Roger's days, their telling, good-natured criticism of the foibles of the time.

"Don't you find your students very much bored by the 'Spectator' papers ?" asked a distinguished academic visitor to our class room. We have heard this question frequently put. We know that in some cases the doubt has been justified; but these were cases in which the papers were mishandled. Sometimes they have been read too early in the first year; at others, too clumsily. They may be made a delightful experience to boys and girls of the third or fourth year. How? By hearty, appreciative reading, (1) creating for heart and mind the engaging, the urbane and gracious, if quaint, personality of Sir Roger, and of the good baronet's friends, taciturn Mr. Spectator, garrulous Will Wimble, and the rest; (2) reconstruction, with amplification from other sources, the social and literary life of London, — its clubs and coffee-houses, its street scenes, theatres, amusements; and (3) similarly reviving for the imagination the country scenes and customs of Old England. It is most important to add Sir Roger to the beloved book-friends of our circle; to enjoy his simple humanity, quiet considerateness, and childlike frankness.

We may open up these large avenues of interest at the outset ; and as we read the papers (some in class, but most at home), collect our data, to be arranged later in outline form. In introducing the papers to our class we may strike the key-note by inviting them to make acquaintance with one of the very few perfect gentlemen of fiction — as she has been called. (Can they think of any others ?) Will they agree with that verdict? If so, by virtue of what qualities ? As we read we shall note any felicities, run down difficult words and allusions, and try to follow the easy flow of the style, — which, when we have concluded our study, we may try to imitate by inventing a new short "Spectator" dissertation of our own.

Of supplementary work there may be as much as one will,— browsings in the "Spectator" at large, with expository summaries of any numbers that may especially strike the fancy; in Steele's letters; in Thackeray, Dobson, and other writers who have thrown enhancing light on the men and the epoch. There may be a map of old London, with coffee-houses, theatres, etc., located. Our literary map of England and Ireland, which we keep on hand and enlarge as new data occur, will be added to; and our chronological tables brought down to Addison's dates.

If we pass on at once to Macaulay's "Essay on Addison," all matters connected with the lives of both Addison and Steele may be taken in connection with that. An effective way of dealing with it and with all works of its kind, as we have found, is this:-

1. Teacher's Introduction: the foreground. Macaulay and his Essays. The Great Reviews and Reviewers.
2. Reading of Essay: so many pages assigned; the student required to underline neatly in pencil the topic matter of each paragraph; the text discussed so as to assure a mastery of the main points.
3. The structure of the whole essay to be shown in a detailed

outline; this involving a second reading, conquering smaller details of allusion, etc.

4. This outline made the basis of a development of detail in topical treatment: (a) The course of Addison's life, especially his political fortunes (involving main facts as to political changes); (b) His literary development and works; (c) His literary friendships and connections, especially his relations with Steele, Pope, and Swift; (d) His character; Macaulay's bias; unfairness to Steele (cf. Thackeray's estimate), etc.

5. The technique of the Essay: management of two strands:-
   - I. Addison's life, and the political life of his time, and
   - II. Addison's works and their qualities; and, lastly,
   - III. Paragraph structure: echoes. Sentences: echoes — Diction — Rhythm — Imagery. Proportion: masses; interruptions and digressions.

As to what shall follow these studies, must again depend upon circumstances. Several alternatives suggest themselves: (1) we may take up briefly the biography of Macaulay (a knowledge of it is required for College entrance), and use freely Trevelyan's entertaining "Life and Letters"; or (2) we may, by way of a contrasting study, read Carlyle's "Essay on Burns"; or (3) we may take a new departure from Macaulay's suggestion that in the De Coverley papers we have the beginnings of the modern novel, and read the "Vicar of Wakefield" in the line of evolution,. or "Esmond," or "The Newcomes," or another; or (4) we may make a thorough change, and introduce here our third Shakespeare play,— "Midsummer Night's Dream," "As You Like It," "Twelfth NIght." An excursion into the field of biographical literature, which shall give an intimation of the really great biographies and autobiographies, will be of great value, if we can make it; so that much may be said for work in (1) or (2). Any of these four studies will be treated after the manner already suggested for the novel or the play; although, of course, there will be some variations, some abbreviating of steps, some advance beyond the steps taken in dealing with former instances. Also we shall have found room for a study of Webster in the course in oratory and debate, — which will come well toward the end of the term, so as to lead on in the beginning of the fourth year to Burke's Speech on "Conciliation."

Thus our fourth year will open then. The treatment of Burke's Speech will resemble that of Macaulay's "Essay on Addison"; only that, as it implies the personal presence of the orator, the scenes and circumstances of the delivery, — historical setting, audience, the issues at stake, — it will involve the taking of a different point of view. Certain imaginative exactions have to be made. Moreover, here we have a great unitary argument; a sort of necessary progression of ideas, — the pressing forward, as with an army of ideas on the march, toward a beleaguered citadel.

We shall begin by reviewing the facts leading up to the delivery of the speech, — facts of American and English history. The student must have a sense of Burke's effort being, from the English point of view, an attempt made, "on the eve," to avert a great disaster; from the point of view of actual occurrences in the Colonies, a pathetic, tragic effort "after the event." This done, we shall begin to read the speech aloud; but once well under way, and the imaginative illusion of speaker and audience secured, we shall dispense with the vocal reading of a great part of it, selecting those passages which patently involve speaker and audience. Each recitation will begin with a summary of what has been read up to date; when the argument, having been resumed, may be carried forward clearly. The topic of each paragraph will be indicated either by underlining or by written condensation *(précis)*. Then a brief will be drawn, showing, besides the careful subordinations of primary, secondary, and tertiary strata in the argument, the broad divisions — introduction, announcement of position and thesis, exposition of data, etc. It is a great mistake, we think, to relieve the student of any part of this work by editorial aids; and we would strongly urge the importance of using a text-book that does not offer these weakening crutches. We know that this is a stiff piece of work, but it is very much worth while. It is in connection with this elaboration of the brief that we shall consider the subject of argument and the syllogism generally, and their leading types; shall take a large outlook over the speech, its logical unity or the absence of it, its proportion, its varying emphasis and climax. Then will follow a detailed study of the parts, as these are set forth in the brief, involving a clearing up of all facts and allusions, including a comprehension of the leading data as to the British Constitution and parliamentary organization and procedure; then a study of the style, literary allusions, and reminiscences; and finally a closer study of Burke, his personality and career, and his other American speeches, — conveniently brought together for us by Professor George (see Heath's edition).

This may cost at least two months of steady work, at the rate of three recitations a week (not including parallel composition work in Argumentation). It is not too high a price to pay. Rapid, slipshod work on such a masterpiece is a folly, an impertinence. We must give the mind time enough to become saturated with it, to react naturally upon it. How great a services may be done to our students , we may better realize if we recall Mr.John Morley's words concerning the three speeches on American affairs, that they are "the most perfect manual in all literature for the study of great affairs, whether for the purpose of knowledge or action,"— great by reason of " the vigorous grasp of masses of compressed detail, the wide illumination from great principles of human experience, the strong and masculine feeling for the two great political ends of Justice and Freedom, the large and generous interpretation of expediency, the morality, the vision, the noble temper." And concerning Burke himself: "There are great personalities like Burke who march through history with voices like a clarion trumpet and something like the glitter of swords in their hands. They are as interesting as

1 "On the Study of Literature," in "Miscellaneous Studies."

their work. Contact with them warms and kindles the mind."[1]

We have scant opportunity to speak about the other fea-tures of the fourth year work. We should pass on now to"Mac-beth," gathering together, with the aid of the notes taken in the three preceding years (an important function of these notes), the large threads of our Shakespearean studies. The work may be less formal, and more abbreviated,— although we would not omit the oral reading of the play, because the ear should be amply accustomed to the free, irregular rhythms and long, large swell of the verse. If we can get our students to apprehend and feel the high seriousness of the play (to use Arnold's terms), the grand style of the verse, the amplitude of the treatment, by way of bringing home the greatness of the issues involved and the large-limbed nature and carriage of Macbeth, — we shall have done the best of good service. The plot may be diagrammed, as we have already suggested, by means of the pyramidal figures employed by Freytag; and there may be a close study of the act and scene structure, the subtle, dramatic patterning of the play. The study in this respect, and also in its supreme interest,— the character development of Macbeth and Lady Macbeth, — may easily lead the enthusiastic teacher into depths beyond the reaches of youthful souls. We must be on our guard against this, and feel our way with tact, suggesting rather than grappling with the ultimate ethical issues involved.

The space-limits imposed upon us in this volume, which we already begin to overstep, prevent our going into further details, and necessitate a brief treatment of remaining features of the work of the fourth year.

After the gloom of the great tragedy it will be a happy change to emerge into the sun light of Milton's "Comus," and enjoy the strains of the pastoral flute and Thyrsis' madrigal. We can make a transition by an excursus on the subject of the his-tory of the drama and the theatre in England, and the rise of the masque. To insure appreciation at once of the lyric blithe-ness of 'Comus," and of the chastened austerity of the high ar-gument in behalf of Virtue, is no easy task. We must not worry the text; there must be a spirit of reserve and delicacy in our handling: plenty of reading, of memorizing, of declamation; and just as much work on the text as is necessary to make it generally intelligible. Let the teacher select the most important points, and see that these are well comprehended. Then we should refer back to "L' Allegro" and "Il Penseroso," and note Milton's growth, especially in the treatment of Nature. Then "Lycidas" may follow, to be treated in the same reserved but admiring fashion. Happy the teacher who can evoke any adequate response in young hearts from so rare a product of the highest poetic workmanship! If he can lodge its lovelier elegiac harmonies in the memory of his students, if he can make it sing itself and its pictures and images, — the high lawns, Lycidas' laureate hearse, the train of mourning figures, the wash of the sounding seas, — so that it may become something of a touchstone of excellence when recalled in later years, he will have done better than well.

Macaulay's "Essay on Milton" may follow, to be treated after the manner of the "Essay on Addison," and the remainder of our time given to one or other of the rounding-out studies suggested in Chapter XIV.[1] We would not be more definite and prescriptive. We have insisted upon the value of plans, and we have nothing to retract on that score in relation to Secondary School work. But while we do well to plan each year's work beforehand, and a scheme of treatment for each book studied, we must be ready to modify these to suit the unexpected development or lack of development on the part of our students. Sometimes we shall linger more than we had arranged to do over this or that piece of work; it will seem worth while with some sets of pupils: at other times we shall run up against dead spots and hurry on.

It all comes back to the necessity of preserving the personal element, keeping the personal touch delicate, and the personal sympathy sensitive at this stage of the work. To be impersonal and general in it, to allow the pupil to escape beyond the radius of heart-to-heart and mind-to-mind contact, is to fail.

---

1. See page 268—9.

3

Composition in the Secondary School

WE shall not in this chapter cover ground already traversed in our chapters on composition in the Primary and Grammar Grades, but, taking for granted the leading principles affecting composition advanced in those chapters, shall try to meet the new circumstances and demands that arise in the Secondary School. What changes in method of attack and in the development of plans are called for, now that we have the adolescent to deal with? Generally, it may be said that the vital distinction between this stage and the preceding stages of our work is that, whereas the emphasis has hitherto been strong upon habituation and uniformity, in the Secondary School stage a new reliance is put upon conscious freedom or self-regulation, and upon developing individual differences and preferences. We have to deal with students who, while much more critical than pupils of the pre-adolescent period, are nevertheless much more accessible and mouldable, much more readily and deeply inspired, than their juniors. In the English work the most important developments are of those nascent emotions referred to in an earlier chapter,— a feeling for style and a capacity for appreciation poetry.

The first essential of real success in composition work is to make proficiency in it seem worth while to our students. This does not mean getting up sensational interest in the work. It does not mean cockering the whims, the passing moods, and flying interests of the student. Nor does it mean working by the fashionable recipe that school is not a preparation for life, but life itself, — a doctrine that too easily tends to sap the vitals of youth and to work havoc among us. The pupil knows better. He discriminates between the life of adult self-direction and vocation which is ahead of him, and the necessary preparation for that life. This preparation will seem worth while, and will even be "good sport" to him, for all its austerities, provided the end is appreciated and the teachers trusted. In this field, as in the field of athletics, the student takes his seat at the training table to make ready for a contest that is ahead. He is doing what others think it right that he should do, to attain ends he cannot fully foresee or appraise. Humility is required of him, and trustful obedience. Let him feel that the wisdom of the ages and the sages — the long experimentation and gathering tradition of centuries — is behind him; and that respect for his elders and betters is his first lesson. He is not in school primarily to please himself; he is there to fulfil his rational human destiny, as his elders interpret it. He is there for work; and he is fortunate if, in doing that work, he gets (as well he may, — and should) a sense of the worth-whileness of it that is a joy and a satisfaction to him.

The moral of which reflections is, that the English teacher will do a great wrong to his students unless his labors with them are touched by something of a spirit of austerity, requiring a serious, self-denying girding of the loins. One may so easily follow the fashion of going too eagerly in quest of the student's so-called "interest," especially at a time when he is prone imperiously to assert them. We have too frequently seen the debilitating effects of such concessions. Instead, it is rather a teacher's business, — sometimes to create interests; sometimes to starve them. His point of view, which he must help his students to take with him, is that of the race and the ages; his outlook, that of civilization and its needs. It is his business to lift his students out of narrow and narrowing grooves of interest, to keep open, as Herbart puts it, the circle of their ideas, and to expand that circle. It is his business to tone his students up with a manly zest, so that they may regard the tasks assigned to them as so many challenges, — ay, as foes resolutely to be wrestled with, if you will. And this attitude does not involve any repression of individuality, which every good teacher rejoices to recognize and foster; it merely means safeguarding true individuality against premature and one-sided expression ; against wilfulness and self-indulgence.

An attitude of this sort is quite consistent with a recognition of the varied incentives to effort that ought to count in English work. There is the utilitarian incentive, — the practical importance of the art of the ready writer; its sheer business value. With one type of student — of the poorer sort undoubtedly — this will have considerable weight; but it should yield to higher motives. There will be no heartiness in work done under its merely prospective influence. It may be supplemented by an appeal to the social motive, to *amour propre* — an appeal that may be most effectively made indirectly by the quiet assumption that refined speech is an indispensable part of good manners and gentle breeding, the safest passport into cultivated society. While this may be preached sometimes from the teacher's desk, it is to be felt chiefly through the teacher's own example and personality; through the spirit and atmosphere of the work. Goodness, as some one has said, is self-diffusive; and so it is with good manners;- they are self-commending; and the teacher who has them, perforce diffuses them.

But these motives to taking pains must not stand in the way of the third, — the princeliest of them all, — a craftsman-like pleasure in the work itself. Nothing less will satisfy the good teacher; he must rouse the linguistic conscience and artistic spirit. To excel in the work must be a point of honourable and cherished ambition. The boy or girl must be happy, his classmates and, above all, his teacher must be happy, over any good piece of language work turned out from the literary shop or workroom, as over any admirable piece of work turned out from the art studio or the machine shop. This or that deft piece of narrative or ingeniously-wrought story; this or that graphic description, flashing a place or a personality upon the mind; this or that crystal-clear exposition or irresistible argument, — should provoke admiration and delight just as an effective piece of wood-carving or bent iron-work or beaten brass does. And it may. We speak out of personal experience in a Manual-training School, where the good literary craftsman was frequently followed in his work with the interest with which the craftsman in wood or iron was followed at the bench or forge; where literary products were overhauled with something of the curiosity and pride shown in overhauling the products of the arts and crafts.

Speaking with no sentimental yearning toward academic Utopia, but on the basis of actual experience and grouping effort, we say deliberately that the trouble with much of our work is that it is too coarsely and too clumsily done. It lacks atmosphere ; it is not pursued either broadly or finely enough, in the spirit of the craftsman. Anything like delight in the making and using of linguistic products is absent from it. The spirit surrounding it is rather that of the factory, where certain marketable, machine-made products are made. rules for good conduct are posted, with a list of fines and penalties. Some of our teachers and text-books speak as if a boy may be drilled and harried into clearness and correctness of speech, as he may be into punctuality or cleanliness. But the important habit of punctuality, if we succeed in establishing it, is a very different matter from a continuing passion for taking pains in self-expression; a continuing scrupulousness, not only to make ourselves understood and to square our expression with our thought, but to carry conviction, and to do justice to our own feelings and ideals. We are dealing with character in a broader and deeper way, not only to initiate and establish fixed habits, but to generate tendencies, — a certain consecutive bent of the nature.

It is true that the teacher of Composition may achieve a certain kind of business success in getting his pupils to write in an orderly and correct and wooden manner, and that he may force the pace in gaining this end; but he will miss the larger educational and disciplinary values in Composition work if he is controlled by this aim. The more or less mechanical results which he achieves may be obtained just as well, or better, by the way, in pressing forward to the greater ends. In the one case, we produce a correct but probably disaffected writer; in the other, with less violent and hurried assault upon carelessness, disorder, and haste, we produce the boy who has something of a way of putting things, — something of a relish and pride in the felicities of his writing. The broader method involves a realization on the teacher's part of the fact that *what he has on his hands in attempting to make of a student a good writer is, first of all, a character, and only secondarily an intelligence and an aptitude.* How if, by his rude daily demand for perfunctory work, his curt "stand and deliver," he should have undermined the finer forces of character, — the love of order, of power, of beauty, of fairness and courtesy, — all of which are involved in the effort to be correct and effective in one's speech?

We shall never get our students to assume the proper attitude toward their work in Composition and Rhetoric unless we can make them feel that in striving for the art of self-expression, they are striving for self-comprehension, self-mastery, and self-origination. We must bring home to them the fact, spreading now in more technical terms, that work in description or narration involves much more than observance of the rules of grammar and rhetorical construction; that it is at once a training of the eye to see, the mind to discriminate its objects and its impressions, the heart to report its feelings of beauty and delight, the conscience and memory to be true to fact; and, similarly, that in exposition and argument they are called upon to do justice to a thesis or idea; to be scrupulous in the presentation of facts; to respect their foes, and be at pains to appreciate a foeman's point of view; and to gain their point fairly by the power of fact, of logic, of truth. It is for these reasons, among others, that we agree heartily with Professor Genung when he says:-

"I have always regarded rhetoric as dealing, in all its parts and stages, with real literature in the making, and composition, however humble its tasks, as veritable authorship, well meant and conscientious. There is no mystery in the literary art or mood which is not present in germ in the efforts of the schoolboy as he writes about the objects of his youthful interest; the difference lies merely in the different stages of mental development and skill. . . . To put the student frankly on the basis of authorship, and respect him accordingly, to impose upon yourself, as his guide and model, a corresponding standard of achievement and culture, is to impart immensely greater reality to his study of rhetoric, and to help him realize, what is the truth, that his exercises in words and sentences are concerned, not with what will soon be superseded, but with constructive principles that must accompany his work to his life's end."

And now for some of the practical consequences of our position, with its stress upon the importance of working, in the spirit of refined artisanship, for character development through self- expression.

If in the class room and conference room we are intent upon these larger values — character values and aesthetic values in conjunction; if we are working for the clear, observing eye, for large, bold ways of conceiving things, for fineness and resonance of sensibility, for moral insight and scrupulousness, — this must mean a liberal amount of individual work with our students; and this means small classes and frequent personal conferences between pupil and teacher. Squad-drill in Composition should be out of the question in Secondary School work. We speak, not with the bias of the specialist, but from the Principal's point of view, when we urge that in no department of the Secondary School will it pay so well to be liberal in the provision of teachers and the limitation of the size of classes as in the English work. The influence a good English teacher may have through effective personal work (as distinguished from hurried squad-work) in the class room, and through the still greater intimacy of the private conference, is incalculable. We will be more definite.

First of all, the work in the class room must permit of much reading aloud of the written work. Every student should be called upon at least twice a month — when, he will not know beforehand. Our classes must not be so large as to preclude this. The seminar method will be approximately followed, more particularly in the third and fourth years. In the class criticism the note of positive appreciation will lead, and fault-finding come after. The teacher will say: "Sewell, that was well-conceived, strongly welded together; or that was finely or sturdily felt, or it had life and movement. What a pity that certain flaws in the workmanship bothered us ! You repeated yourself there, and weakened your effect. There you bungled or missed a strong antithesis. You were ambiguous or confused in one place. You threw us off the scent by an irrelevancy. You misused a word. It was clear, from your confusion in reading at such a point, that you had not punctuated. You must not allow these things to discount your good effects."

It is after the papers have been handed in that the teacher, in the privacy of the conference room, will find that opportunity kindly to rebuke and rally which delicacy denied to him in the publicity of the class room. "Your work is full of feeling — a valuable asset; but it is seriously discounted by mental incoherence. See here and here. Or, "Your work indicates a failing that will cripple you through life, if not battled with; you are carelessly inaccurate. Things are not as you represent them. Either you have not been conscientious enough to look closely and patiently at your object, or you have not been at pains to find words for what you saw. Your loose use of words implies either indolence or a crude, slap-dash way of thinking." Or, again, "Your letter to your friend was dashing, but a trifle self-magnifying or lacking in considerateness; and see, he well be obliged to read this passage twice, because the absence of punctuation marks or this ambiguity will puzzle him." There is no need to enlarge upon the deep impressions for good that may be made upon a student by means of these friendly and intimate talks over the "business" of writing. A boy's or girl's work in Composition opens innumerable doors into the heart and mind and conscience.

The next point to be insisted upon in the organization of the Composition work is that of giving practical effect to a view generally taken by good teachers, but too seldom acted upon, — that students shall be expected in any written work done in the

Secondary School (and we would add oral work, were that possible) to live up to the standards exacted by the English Department, and that they shall in some way be held to account for their shortcomings. We know too well the difficulties in the way of putting this pious theory into practice. The special teachers have no time, — frequently have no inclination, — sometimes no skill, to enforce the rule. On the other hand, it is not possible that all written work should pass muster before the English Department. What then? Shall the effort be altogether abandoned as impracticable? Not at all; the matter is too important. We must consider it more carefully.

As we have said in an earlier chapter, the important requirement is that whenever the student is engaged in the act of composition, — that is, whenever he is expressing himself, — he must feel bound to be accurate in his way of saying things, whatever the subject may be or whatever the nature of the exercise he is engaged upon. More injurious, perhaps, than anything else to a student's powers of expression, is the distinction he draws between the work done for the English Department as a set exercise in Composition, and work done for the history teacher or the classics teacher, as the case may be, to test his knowledge. The student thereby sets up two linguistic standards, and develops two linguistic selves. He sets off the work in Composition as something apart, — something in which peculiar endeavour and a special scrupulousness are expected. In some schools so much written work is required, that it is impossible that it should be well or even carefully done. The Composition teacher is apt to forget that, in addition to his own special written work, the students have many written tasks for other teachers. It is quite as important, indeed it is more important, that these should be creditably done, than that the composition work of the English Department should be. Far better were it in such circumstances for the English teacher to say to his class: "To-morrow you have an account of the battle of Thermopylae, or the Roman Praetorship, to write for your history teacher; I have arranged with him that this essay shall serve the purpose also of the English Department." Or, again, "I find that to-day you had a written review or test in Cicero, and that it included the translation of a passage from the 'De Senectute.;' The Latin teacher will hand the papers to me, after he has seen them, and I shall go over them from the point of view of the specialist in English." Other ways of dealing with the problem may suggest themselves; but the point here insisted upon is, that, somehow or other, the students must feel that the English Department does concern itself with the work done in all departments, by way of enforcing the general principle stated above. It may be by descending at times upon the several departments in turn, and gathering a select crop of papers; or by making special arrangement for periodical returns from each. It has been our good fortune to work with teachers in other departments with whom there was an understanding in this regard. We would receive from them weekly, or less frequently, papers that obviously required attention from the English Department; and, at stated intervals, batches of papers from the whole class, for supplementary criticism on the language side. The least that the English teacher can do is to keep informed as to what written work his classes are doing in other departments, and what problems in expression it presents. One other point in this connection; that is, the importance of establishing uniform requirements in all departments as to the form and quality of written work, — paper and ink, headings, margins, indorsements, etc.

It is at this juncture that, casting an eye over the sum of written work that is being done by our students, we find ourselves involved once more in a recognition of the fact that they are continually called upon to produce compositions of all kinds, — narrative, descriptive, expository, argumentative. Returns from other departments will bring this out. From which it follows that, in attending to one particular kind of composition and a special set of problems at one time in the English Department, we cannot exclude altogether some attention to the other kinds and to general problems. The necessity of having a method, and of achieving a progressive and methodical conquest of the difficulties of writing, will involve us in placing an emphasis for the time being upon this or that kind. Such particularization in the English field may be likened to intensive work upon special periods in the field of History. A certain large and general view of the whole subject is taken for granted, while step by step a closer and more careful view and treatment of a certain part of the field is gained. It is well to remember also that before our students reach the Secondary School, they have been workers in the field at large, and may have worked intensively upon some parts of it.

Allowing, then, for the fact that, while engaged upon the intensive cultivation of a particular species of composition, we have these larger aims to pursue, we may elaborate our plan of dealing successively in three or four years of our course with the four species, — Narration, Description, Exposition and Argument. We would begin at once with the work of writing short, and at intervals, lengthier narratives — incidents of personal life, stories remembered, episodes from books of travel, adventure, and biography; reductions of long stories, novels and poems. There are those who prescribe a year of introductory work — partly review, and partly a survey of general principle governing Composition in general; some grammatical considerations; rules as to choice of subject, diction, sentence, paragraphs, etc. We have put this plan to the proof, and have found it less successful than the one we now advocate. In the first place it does not give that sense of a fresh beginning which is so important. Let our students feel now that their Composition work is to be done on a higher plane, — on the basis of rhetoric principle. Explain what rhetoric means; bring home the distinction between it and Grammar. Let them feel that a working knowledge of Grammar is to be presupposed — however sorely some of them may need brushing up in it.

This method of procedure does not mean, however, that we shall at once begin to load up with rhetorical principles and rules. No. We would proceed with Rhetoric in the Secondary School as we proceeded with Grammar in the Elementary School. We would discover, register, and apply our rules in the process of our practice, proceeding from the art to the science.

We begin at once to learn to do by doing, and not by a laborious mastery of tools. We shall get help from models and from judicious criticism, but we shall at once be involved in the elaboration of certain simple principles that are involved in our actual work. We might suggest to our pupils that the simplest thing to be done is to be able to answer their parents' or friends' endlessly repeated questions, 'What have you to tell me? What of importance or interest has happened to you to-day or lately? Give an account of yourself. Let's have your story." Here is a real task : why not excel in it ? Why not see to it that the story (narration) is clear, has a point (idea, climax), and hangs together (unity): that, if possible, it is interesting and entertaining (style). "See, — this is the sort of thing, — this little sketch from Bunner or Daudet or Stevenson or Hawthorne (a note from one of the' Note-books,' perhaps). Now recall or hunt up something similar you have heard or read. Try your hand at telling a friend in a letter of something that has happened to you recently. Give an imaginary narrative (oral) to your father in reply to his evening inquiry for the news of the day." In some such way we may get started with the real and stimulating business — alas ! to some only : to others it is the still boresome business — of writing, instead of the with tiresome exercises in how to choose a subject, how to abbreviate, how to arrange a complex sentence, and what not.

We have one more important reason for proceeding in this way; it is the reason that is leading us away — as recent text-books show — from the old synthetic method of proceeding, from the parts to the whole, from a study of bricks and mortar, rooms and floors, instead of from a plan of the whole edifice, and working down to the constituent parts and the required materials. The old method, beginning with words, proceeded to sentences; advanced then to paragraphs, and finally to the whole composition. The new method begins with the large, if inchoate thought that is to articulate itself in a paragraph or a group of paragraphs, and works down into the parts as they are conditioned by the purpose and spirit of the whole. It is an illustration once more of the counsel of the artist, — "Get in your masses first; settle your details afterward, and let them determine themselves through the attempt to create a whole, and to convey a total meaning and impression."

Let it be admitted that there is difficulty in working out this method consistently. The advocate of the old method may well urge that in paying so much attention to the larger features of composition work, there is danger of loose dealing with those faults in the use of words, spelling, sentences, construction, and so on, which the student will commit. We cannot, as a matter of practice, ignore those mistakes, or postpone the treatment of them in detail, until we have mastered the art of planning and executing the larger elements of composition. Very true, we answer; there must, after all, be something of a combination of the two methods. But we should insist upon starting at the big end of the plank. We should start by getting our students to envisage in a large way the subject upon which they intend to write, and to articulate its parts gradually, down to the smaller divisions. If it is urged, in rejoinder, that there ought at least to be preliminary work on the sentence, seeing that "sentence-sense" is so fundamental in composition, — we would reply that the sentence as an isolated unit is unknown in composition, save in the form of the proverb. The sentence is always the servant — ay, the child — of the paragraph; and the education of the feeling for the sentence necessarily involves its being studied as a part of the larger whole in which it has its strictly determined function. By and by there may be a review of the whole subject from the synthetic point of view in a brief course in formal Rhetoric, just as there was a review of Grammar at the conclusion of the Elementary School course.

The parallelism between the courses in Grammar and Rhetoric will hold in still another particular — the use of text-book in Composition and Rhetoric may be used for reference and for occasional exercises, but for little else. The chief desiderata in such a book are a simple summarizing of the leading principles, copious illustrations, and judicious exercises. Let there be a good working class-room collection of the standard books, to which the students may be referred for guidance on particular points. But we have come to believe that our prime task as teachers of Composition and Rhetoric is to bring home to our students how inevitably the art of writing and the science underlying it develop of themselves in and through the orderly, progressive practice of writing. It is upon this practice, and not upon a text-book, that we must rely to develop needs : the text-book may be used to meet these needs ; not to forestall or create them.

A text-book may also perform the valuable service of rough- charting a course along which the teacher may guide his pupils; and we are assuming that the teacher will so steady himself by the best text-books, and get from them all the help he can in his voyaging. The pupil must not be allowed to feel that he is merely drifting. He must perceive a continuity in the stages of the progress; and the teacher must provide for this. And yet his students will learn to write much as an art student learns to paint; by getting to work in the master's studio and taking the master's cues. He will "catch on," will do largely by instinct what the master will know how to justify by theory, until, by and by, an implicit theory emerges out of and steadies the practice. He will accept the master's aid in determining what to do first, on what to concentrate for the time being and what for the nonce to slight or postpone — be it special problems of form, composition, color, values, atmosphere. The master decides that, for the time being, *this* special difficulty must be mastered, as a condition of the next step forward ; *that* one left until this is conquered. Without pressing the analogy between two arts, which, while having broad principles in common, differ much in details of method, we may state how, as it seems to us, the four years' work in Composition should be charted.

Our plan is to distribute the technical difficulties of writing as far as possible according to the sharpness and urgency with which they emerge in dealing successively with the four species of Composition. It is clear, for example, that narration involves preeminently the problems of structure in their simplest form;

that description brings into more striking clearness problems of diction ; exposition, problems of definition and clearness; while argument involves the consideration of force and fact. Argument indeed conducts us from the domain of Rhetoric to that of Logic, and involves such severities of thought and of skill in construction, that we cannot proceed for with it in the Secondary School.

Narration is so much easier to manage than any other form of composition, that it gives us the best chance to deal with certain elementary and general problems of form and technique. It is the most objective species of literary composition; the writer feels the firm hold of fact and of the simple logic of sequence upon him. Required to move from a definite starting-point to an unmistakable goal, — a simple conclusion in the case of the plotless narrative; a climax, where there is plot, — his task is to mark the larger stages of progression; to paragraph these; to attend to his paragraph echoes and links; to knit well together his component sentences, on the same principle of carrying forward the action step by step, steadily and surely, sentence by sentence, without the endless, dragging chain of the "and" the "but" formation. The students mind is to be kept to the story, his sentence formations — long and short, loose or periodic — corresponding with the nature of the incident, its length or brevity, slowness or swiftness. It is the simplest type of sentence and paragraph — the loose — that is called for; and the punctuation is correspondingly simple. Simplicity, in fact, a sound straightforwardness, is what is primarily demanded. Wordiness and irrelevancy can be easily detected and demonstrated. The fundamental principles of Unity, Mass, Coherence, Sequence, are seen on a large and convincing scale, and appreciated as they cannot be on a small scale in the sentence, — to which they may now be the more easily applied. As the weight of attention will fall on the logic of incident, the scenic interest and character interest, which involve descriptive work, will be permitted only when such descriptive enlargements are necessary to develop the action. The most conspicuous result of this first stage of our work should be a gain in vigor and precision.

We have already suggested the various forms which Narration may take — personal experience and anecdote in letter and diary; invention in supplying the conclusion of an unfinished tale, or in making variants upon a given story, or in the complete weaving of one. We have also insisted that the work should go hand in hand with the study of models in the literature class, supplemented by special studies in the composition class. We will add here only a recommendation of plenty or work in reduction and expansion. Let the student reduce to the lowest terms the plots of some of Hawthorne's tales ; and let the teacher call for the expansion of a reduction made by himself from some short story unknown to his class. Well-chosen newspaper reports may be treated in the same way. Biography also lends itself to these exercises in economy and condensation.

The work in Description, at the outset of the second year, brings us face to face with a new set of problems. We believe in raising these problems in the sharpest way by considering at the outset the two types of description, — scientific and literary; description for information and explanation, and description for impression and enjoyment. This may be done by comparing examples such, let us say, as those brought into happy juxtaposition by Professor Genung; a guide-book description of Avignon from the Cyclopaedia, and an impressionistic description from Felix Gras' "The Reds of the Midi." ("The Working Principles of Rhetoric," pp. 16-17.) Following this line of treatment, it may be brought home to the student that in writing a letter of direction to a friend, a diagram of streets and roads will be much more effective in enabling his friend to find his way than a verbal explanation will be. Similarly, the verbal description of an object for identification (a police specification, *e.g.*) will differ from one for appreciation. We shall work out this difference in concrete instances; and in doing so, we shall have to take into account all the vital considerations concerning descriptive writing; the point of view, the selection of the salient and focal features, the order and grouping of them to the end of economizing the reader's attention, and so on. We shall be led to discriminate between the objective character of the scientific or explanatory description (the truth of external fact) and the subjective character of the impressionistic and appreciative description (seeking truth of subjective impression); between the denotative diction demanded by the one and the connotative, suggestive diction required by the other.

Let there be plenty of this comparative work. Let the student attempt both modes. Let him transform a scientific enumeration or analysis made in the laboratory into literary description. Read to him or dictate the passage wherein Mr. Stedman contrasts the weather bureau report of an approaching storm with two stanzas of verse reflecting the storm as it sweeps down upon the northern ports, lashes the headlands, and pours its furious armies into bays. Discuss examples from Darwin and Huxley, Burroughs and Jefferies, books of travel and exploration, books of verse, especially Tennyson's descriptive poems. That is the way to give meaning and interest to the work. A treatment of the Synonym, Simile, Metaphor, will be involved in this. We shall find, as we go, the need of greater skill and variety in sentence-formation, and of more varied punctuation. The significance of rhythm and onomatopoetic effect in literary description will become plain. Finally, descriptive work in verification will be asked for.

We have always found great value in the attempt to lead our students to see wherein description in words differs from the artist's description in colour and form. What is it that words cannot give at all, or give but weakly ? Shape, colour, sound. What can they do that no other vehicle can compass so well ? Change, movement, succession — the suggestion, intimation, comparison. Examine with the pupils some of the prolix descriptions attempted occasionally by writers — even Scott. Note how much better the end might have been gained by a sketch or picture. A flood of light may be let in by this method. Students may be brought to most helpful sense of what they may legitimately attempt by the verbal method of description. This is not advanced work : it comprises the very elements of the subject. The teacher must, of course, be familiar with the distinctions drawn in Aesthetics between the time arts and the space arts, and with the gist of Lessing's famous discussion of the subject in the "Laocoon."

When some skill has been acquired, there may be a return to the narrative, with a view to an amalgamation of the two kinds, and an expansion — in cases where it is absolutely required — of the narrative by descriptive adjuncts of character, scenery, and circumstance.

How shall we most effectively begin our intensive labors in Exposition ? By reverting to its kinship with Description ; by showing that it is merely a development of Description of the explanatory, enumerative species. We may compare Ruskin's celebrated description of the locomotive, or Thoreau's brief, impressionistic picture of it, with such an expository description as that by Holmes in Lamont's "Specimens of Exposition" (Holt). To avoid confusion, it will be well to bring out strongly the differences rather than the affinities between the two types. Our models will be as distinctive as possible, emphasizing especially the fact that, whereas Description gives us things as they appear to be, as they affect the senses and the mind through the senses, Exposition deals with as they *are* for thought, "as conceived and organized in thought," to use Professor Genung's phrase; exhibiting their anatomy and their functioning, and rationalizing these so that they may be — must be — understood by any reasonable person. We are to try to get beyond what is particular, individual, and unique in the object and the impression produced by it, to what is general and common. We must get ourselves out of the way first of all, — our idiosyncracies of feeling and expression must be banished ; and then we must not allow our interest to be centered on what is peculiar or strange, unusual or abnormal, in the thing we are dealing with. Splendid discipline this, both of mind and character!

We shall therefore press on to the means by which we reach this result : definition; analysis, with an understanding of genus, species, and differentia ; simplification and explication by repetition, description, or illustration ; distinction by antithesis or contrast, obversion, analogy and comparison. We shall then deal in a new and closer way with terms, and handle words with severer scrutiny ; weigh synonyms, antonyms, homonyms, ambiguities equivocations, etc.; the denotation and connotation of words ; the literary and scientific modes of employment.

Following our usual method, these different matters will be dealt with as we go, and not developed at any length rhetorically before we get down to work. It is a good plan to begin with models, and to reduce them to outline form ; to summarize, epitomize, and at times paraphrase or metaphrase them. In original work we may begin simply, with subjects carefully delimited ; and it is here, where it becomes fully significant, that this problem of the delimitation of the topic should be studied, and not before. General propositions involving no great complexity of treatment, and no extended research, will serve best,—topics involving definition and discussion rather than propositions involving the forestalling of objections. Then we shall go into methods of treatment. The processes to be gone through will be something like this :-

1. Taking stock of one's own ideas and knowledge ; overhauling it, and so realizing the gaps in one's knowledge and the cloudiness in one's thoughts, etc.
2. Rough sketch of a plan of treatment on the basis of one's present knowledge; making the best of this, and getting it provisionally organized.
3. Getting new thought and knowledge, and verifying old ; consulting dictionary, encyclopaedia, and standard authorities. Taking notes on our reading.
4. Revision and expansion of the first sketch in the light of the new facts and ideas ; involving us in the selection and rejection of material available. Decision as to scale of treatment ; proportion.
5. Final; arrangement and development :-

   (1) The larger masses. (2) Detailed outline, providing for subordinate elements. Special attention to beginning (announcement of theme) and conclusion, with its summary, if one is desirable.

There will be class exercises in several of these processes : delimitation of general topics ; provisional outlines made on the basis of present information and ideas ; discussion and elaboration by the class; revised outlines on the basis of the new information and suggestions contributed by the class. Then, after concluding criticisms and suggestions by the teacher, the same topics or others may be assigned for home treatment after further research and more careful consideration.

The transition from Exposition to Argument is natural, inevitable. It means a change from explanation to advocacy; form non-committal to partisanship; from the setting forth in an orderly manner of something that is so, to the establishing of something that is not conceded, but must by proven and carried. Here there is a right and a wrong, or at least a better and a worse; and we are the challenging or challenged champions of what we believe to be the right, the better. Our forces must be ranged in battle array; properly placed and supported with a view to the nature and resources and probable tactics of the other side. We may trace a certain analogy between Narration and Description, and Exposition and Argument, respectively, in this wise : Exposition, like Narration, presents a series of stages along a prescribed route with a goal at the end, each stage being naturally sequent upon the preceding one ; whereas in Argument, as in Description, we have not a straight, sectioned road to traverse; but rather a labyrinth to thread, a pattern to weave, a settled point of view to keep; — in fine, there must be a scheme of reasoning upon which the ordering and presentation of our facts depend. Each stop forward has to be taken cautiously and circumspectly, with an eye to the total effect ; and must be safeguarded from surprise and attack. Then there must be advance into the opponents's territory; and plans to surprise and disarm or to discomfort and rout, must be carefully laid.

The way must be opened by a little systematic work, with models before us, on the nature and processes of argument ; the syllogism and enthymeme; induction and deduction; hypothesis, inference, and proof; attack and refutation by *reduction ad ab-*

surdum and otherwise. Then we shall enter on debate, on the basis of the carefully prepared brief, holding our debaters strictly to account in following it; in the course of which our first modicum of theory will be developed. We shall call periodically for briefs and for the whole or parts of a speech, — sometimes before and sometimes after delivery. We shall require the whole class occasionally to write certain parts of a speech on a given theme,- either openings, refutations, conclusions, or perorations; these being general exercises for the development of readiness and effectiveness. The work may be lightened occasionally by exercises in the humorous, ironic, or epigrammatic manners, — if the teacher can trust himself to keep such work within proper bounds.

These things become possible only if we keep the work simple and vital. It is a great mistake to go far afield in either Exposition or Argumentation and Debate (especially in the latter) into large and, to the students, remote questions of public and political controversy. That well be the tendency ; boys and girls would be men and women before their time. But the chief reason why we should rein the Pegasus of youth in this matter is that we shall be missing a great opportunity to bring our students to close quarters with the problems of personal and educational life which they ought to be revolving, and do fitfully revolve at this time. We can teach them to grapple with these pertinent problems in a thorough and systematic, instead of a slipshod, haphazard way. We can induce a habit of reflection and sober second-thinking, a desire to interrogate ready-made opinion and unexamined prejudice ; we can help to check hasty generalizations, and demonstrate the necessity of consulting precedent and adducing proof and illustration; we can correct the callow egotism of the intellectual fledgling; and above all, we can give dignity and meaning to the interests and everyday affairs of youth. Our work will be, not for display, but usefulness. We shall have on our hands the important business of helping to form and clarify the public opinion of the school.

In the course of the work on Argumentation and Debate, there will be opportunity for using and reviewing in all the other kinds of Composition. Exposition is, of course, involved first of all; and the method of the analytical outline will be that followed in the preparation of the brief, although the brief will permit of parenthetical annotations, for help; in speaking, which the expository outline will not include. The appeal to the feelings involved in the attempt to persuade will, it will early be discovered, require skill in illustration, description and narration. And, as distinctive features, considerations of rhythm and verbal effectiveness, of dignity and impressiveness, of elevation yet variety of tone (where, by the way, we shall have to deal in particular with the balanced construction), will occupy us on the side of formal Rhetoric.

And now, in bringing our treatment to a close, we must — omitting many matters of not unimportant detail — mention some general points.

First, as to class methods. The skilful management of class discussion by the teacher is the most vital factor in the situation. We have urged that there should be plenty of reading of the students' productions. Each should feel that he may be called on at any recitation to read what he has written, for the judgment of his classmates. It is they, his peers, rather than his teacher, who are to be for him as he writes his audience and critics. Behind them will stand for his imagination, as final appraiser, judge, and court of appeal, the figure of his teacher, of whom he should think as holding him to his very best, as following his every step in progress, as demanding evidence of his having profited by all the help received. The class discussion ought to be the most valuable of aids. Next in importance (though prior in time) is the preliminary discussion in the class of the topics assigned for home work. The teacher's directions as to the kind of composition desired ought to be adequate; and often it may be desirable to probe the topic in a broad, suggestive way so as to stimulate thought and open up possible methods of treatment, available models, and sources of information.

As to the teacher's correction of work handed in to him, he must be careful not to overdo correction: that discourages; and so does much rewriting. Some of the more serious and significant blunders and shortcomings may be written on the board to be corrected on the spot, or otherwise. Errors in spelling and punctuation may be similarly treated; and — let it on no account be forgotten — special excellences brought to the notice of the class. Of course, these aids must not be lavish and constant, and must not weaken the students' power to walk alone. Errors below a certain percentage may be corrected on the paper or on a separate sheet. The student or the teacher should keep all compositions for the sake of reference. When a student is doing unusually poor work, the teacher should seek for the deeper, hidden causes, psychological or physical; and aid in remedying them rather than their innumerable results in the defective compositions.

As to the form of the work, and the cultivation of the sense of form, we have already declared our opinions on the point. (See pp. ***) Rules will help but little; we must work in a larger way for an organic appreciation of comeliness, order, and expressiveness by spacing and arrangement, pagination, margination, indention, paragraphing, titling. We may try to arouse a sense for clear, formal handwriting as we should for artistic printing. A few specimens of old manuscripts may help. Perhaps an old leisurely dignity may not be beyond recall. We may war against modern rush and flurry.

Finally, we would emphasize the importance of working for sincerity, of escaping, that is, from conventional, ready-made ways of speaking and writing; of commending individuality in seeing and reporting, or, in the case of natures of an imitative case, individual admiration, — a boy's loving pupilage to a favourite author, — so only they be genuine and heartfelt. Let us hail differences gladly, keeping our own preferences out of the way, and emphasizing them only when there is a call for the championship of the noble against the petty, the real against the sham. The most fatal of results — and a not infrequent one — is when boys write what they think will please the teacher and will jog with his views and whims. The best of results is where, along with an initial humility in the presence of greatness, we can secure a bold reliance upon the truth as our young scholars see it, and that independence of spirit which scorns prevarication and make-believe, the cheap pose and flippant jest.

4

Versification in the Secondary School

THE course in versification is, as we have already intimated, an integral and vital part of the English work, and not a mere fringe upon it. The ends which are to be gained by it are, (1) a deepened appreciation of poetry in and through the attempt to fashion quasi-poetic products, — again an attempt to teach through self-activity; (2) a development of the power to distinguish between the peculiar "notes" of poetry and of prose, — that is, between, discourse suffused and heightened with emotion, and discourse pitched in the lower key of prose writing; and (3), with this, a craftsman-like way of handling words ingeniously, — to manipulate inversions, to scrutinize vocabulary closely, and to command synonyms and rhyme words; and (4) developing this literary tactfulness, by learning to employ simile, metaphor and other figures, alliteration and onomatopoeia, where they may be legitimately employed to gain certain common literary effects— light or stately, tripping or slow-footed, humorous or grave.

It is necessary, of course, at the very outset to put the students at a right point of view by explaining to them these purposes. There is to be no attempt to make poets, any more than there is to make great painters by the work in drawing, painting, and modelling.

The class is to understand that, much as the boys in the old English Grammar Schools wrote (and still write) Latin verse to show their mastery of Latin quantity and the elementary rules of Latin composition and versification; so they, too, are to give evidence of a certain accuracy and facility in the handling of their mother-tounge, of an ear for word-music, and of a reminiscent appreciation of the work of the poets studied. Experience has shown us that there need be little or no fear of any injurious effects: but that, on the contrary, very excellent results may be obtained, — chief among them, a new zest in the English work, and a great deal of innocent and refined pleasure through the invigorating effort to scale the low foot-hills of Parnassus.

An essential condition of success is system in the work. There must be a basis of systematic work in scansion ; and then the progressive study and production of verse forms in their increasing complexity. We will deal first of all with the work in scansion.

Scansion is to be regarded as a method of indicating by a system of signs, how verse is to be read aloud. It is a means of training the ear. The pupils are to show by the use of this notation the accent or rhythm, the quantity and the tempo, of the lines. In order that this may be done, however, there must be certain changes in the methods ordinarily employed, and, indeed, a better technical understanding of English verification than is usually shown in our text-books. For example, it will not do to start from the principle that the basis of English versification is accent merely. Quantity or duration is an important element, and must also be taken into account. Our system will accordingly make allowance for the spondee and pyrrhic as well as the iambus, the trochee, and other kinds of feet mentioned in text-books and treatises; for the reason that a foot is frequently made up of two equally accented syllables, — sometimes heavy (spondee) and sometimes light (pyrrhic). Moreover, due allowance must be made for the irregularities of English verse, the impossibility, that is, of scanning the higher products of English poetry by any uniform sing-song method. The student must be made to feel at the very outset that verse when it is passionate is, as Ruskin says, 'made more beautiful by certain modes of transgression of the constant law" exemplified in the normal lines. Unless the pupils feel the changing pulsation of the verse, realizing that the music varies with the rise and fall of the passion, then we shall have that wooden and valueless scansion that actually damages the ear and beclouds the poetic perception. A very good text to follow is this paragraph from Ruskin's "Elements of English Prosody" :-

"The measures of verse, while their first simple function is to please by the sense of rhythm, order, and art, have for second and more important function that of assisting, and in part compiling, clearness of utterance; thus enforcing with noble emphasis, noble words; and making them, by their audible symmetry, not only emphatic, but memorable."

If we follow this clew, and adopt a suitable method, we shall find that our students are undergoing an education not only of their musical sense, but of their poetic nature, their power of feeling, their capacity for passion, — which is of far greater importance.

Let us at once illustrate what we mean by our contention that a regard must be had for quantity as well as for accent in English verse. Suppose that our students are in their first year reading Shakespeare's "Julius Caesar." It is the passage in which Cassius is attempting to rouse Brutus's feelings against Caesar:-

"Why, man, he doth bestride the narrow world
Like a Colossus; and we petty men
Walk under his huge legs and peep about . ."

How impossible to scan these lines according to any regular iambic plan. The student, in order to indicate by his notation how the passage should be read, will have to employ other signs.[1] He will mark his lines like this :-

Why man | | he doth | bestride | the nar | row world
Like a | Colos | sus | | and | we pet | ty men

1 We have tried, for simplicity, to make the one set ordinarily used serve. We need two: one for accent and one for quantity. Note difficulty in case of "*mel*-ancholy" (below), and "Liberty" (next p.).

Walk un | der his | huge legs | and peep | about. . . .

So too, if we are reading, let us say, Milton's "L'Allegro," a similar effort must be made to indicate the variations upon the normal iambic tetrameter line, and — a more difficult matter — the irregularities of the ten introductory lines which are so full of musical expressiveness. We shall want the pupil to feel (and to show in his scansion) the forceful staccato effect in that opening energetic dismissal of loathed melancholy, with the emphatic force of the word "loathed" :-

Hence, loath | ed mel | ancholy.

What a metrical absurdity the line becomes when read as regular iambic trimeter. It is difficult to indicate the light stress on "mel." And so with the fifth line that gives us more of the same sense of emphatic and energetic power :-

Find out | some un | couth cell.

Not only effects of this kind with their heavy trailing emphasis, but the very opposite light effects of the tripping lines, —

Come, | and trip | it as | you go, |
On | the light | fantas | tic toe |

must be appreciated, and it may be desirable to indicate, in words, the changes from "slow" to "quick," "stately" to "tripping," and so on. Thus, in the lines that follow, we must be sensitive to the change in word values which betokens the touch of seriousness in the thought :-

And in | thy right | hand lead | with thee
The moun | tain nymph, | sweet Lib | erty;

noting the beautiful emphasis secured by the strong "right hand," followed by the rich vowel effects of "lead" and "thee"; and again in the next line, the full values of "mountain nymph" and "sweet." To miss these things is to miss what alone gives value to the exercises in scansion.

This is no place to attempt to set forth at length the views on English versification implied in the position taken above; and what we have said must suffice. On any other basis, the writer would not regard it as worth while to bother his students with scansion. It is, for him, a means of cultivating an appreciation of the musical and passional expressiveness of great poetry.

And now we may indicate the lines upon which our progressive studies of verse forms should proceed. In order that the student may not be hampered by the difficulty of rhyme at the beginning, our first exercise may be in blank verse, taken in connection with some blank-verse poem, that we are studying. Let us suppose that it is the selections from Bryant's translation of the 'Odyssey," the "Ulysses among the Phaecians" before mentioned. We may give the class a start by proposing a subject, and providing a first line. The subject is to be "The Sirens"; the moment chosen being when they sang their luring songs to Ulysses as he and his sailors sailed by their dread abode; or, if the students prefer, the sailors may be Jason and his Argonauts (the writer once read to his class William Morris's dialogue between the Sirens and Orpheus). It will not do to pitch the note too high, and so an introductory line like this may be suggested :-

> And as they neared the shore they heard the songs

and if a second line is desirable, we may continue :-

> Of Sirens sweetly singing from the bay . . . .

The class will be asked to suggest the next line; and by means of suggestion and criticism, we may build up a little stanza of five or six lines that will have served to give courage and stimulus to our young craftsmen. Let them now be asked to take either the same subject or any other and produce a dozen lines or so. Of course, there will be all sorts of ludicrous bungling; but it will all be worth while. To many the work will be a first revelation of the charm and significance of verse.

The advance from blank verse to the couplet and the quatrain is a natural step forward. The quatrain we have found it convenient to take in connection with the study of Gray's "Elegy"; the couplet, when Goldsmith's "Deserted Village" is studied. A simple exercise in connection with Gray is to attempt a description of morning twilight hours and sunrise, with the sounds and sights common to country life at dawn. The subject is discussed, and various experiences are contributed, and, almost before it is aware, the class has on hand a stock of material which may be worked up into verse form. Similarly with Goldsmith's "Deserted Village." The exercise may be an attempt to describe some deserted building or spot which the students have known, or some person or place after the manner of the descriptions of the village parson and schoolmaster in Goldsmith's poem.

At this point we may begin the study of the more formal and compact types of poem. We have usually begun with that dainty form of French verse, the triolet, — a copious supply of models for which may be found in the little volume of "Ballades and Rondeaus" in the Centerbury Poets, compiled by Mr. Gleason White. In fact, it may be well to take this form, and to work it before the quatrain and couplet are handled. Here again, of course, the results will be anything but satisfactory; the dainty triolet will be so roughly handled that the teacher's taste and conscience will be sorely tried. It will be well, as a first exercise, to give a motive or subject, and to supply the first two lines; for example, if we should be working at the time on Milton's shorter poems, we may take a cue from "L'Allegro" and "Il Panseroso"; we have also used the "Merchant of Venice" and secured creditable triolets on Portia, setting as a first line —

Love laughed in her eyes. . . .

The triolet may lead on into the single quatrain embodying an epigram. Models may be drawn from William Watson, Landor and Emerson. After this the progression may be successively through the sextain, the octette *(ottava rima)*, the Spenserian stanza, and, finally, the sonnet. We have managed to secure a passable sonnet from about fifty per cent of our senior class.

If circumstances favor, along with these exercises we may work in a little imitative work, a ballad or narrative poem at times, and a few parodies, using Bayard Taylor, Owen Seaman, and other masters in this line. Now the class will produce its class song, and sometimes verses for special commemorative occasions, — Memorial Day, Christmas, May Day, etc.

Such in brief is the plan we ourselves have followed. Without some such course in versification, we regard the work in English as lacking one important means of culture, and one efficient aid in securing good results in linguistic expression.

5

The Question of Formalism in Method

WHAT we have to say in these supplementary or summarizing words on method is said as the result of experience, not along in teaching boys and girls in the Elementary School and the Secondary School, but also in the teaching and training of teachers, including teachers of the higher and lower grades in our public schools.

The chief burden of our counsel, — when we are asked for an opinion on the subject, — is that what we chiefly need for the improvement of our English teaching is a broader, richer, and more thorough literary training and culture for our teachers. It must be insisted that they shall be exemplary in their habits of speech, capable and interesting readers and writers; well schooled — concretely and practically schooled — in the principles of Rhetoric and Criticism, so that they may know and feel good literature when they see it; generally well read in the great classics (absolutely necessary to the formation of taste and judgment), and in the history of, at least, English Literature. We may take for granted the possession of those general attainments — disciplining power, sympathy, patience, etc. — which are essential in a teacher of anything; there being no need for special emphasis upon any of these qualities in connection with; English teaching unless it be the possession of imaginative sympathy with the child, — the power to take the child's point of view in the sphere of imagination, fancy, illusion, make-believe, to be myth-maker, fetich-worshipper, idolater, play-actor, with him. To do this is difficult, we know, and implies that love of children and childhood which is the one infullible mark of the true teacher; but we shall not enlarge upon this familiar idea.

If we do not lay stress upon the need of a new methodology, upon more psychology, child-study, Herbartian lore, and the obstetrics of pedagogy generally, it is not because we are insensible of the value of these things. We rate them high; but we hold that the clamorous need of the hour, so far as English teaching is concerned, is, above all, a more adequate culture, a sound elementary knowledge and practice of English, the possession of linguistic power, refinement, and liking.

We regret the large proportion of time that is often lavishly spent on the study of *how* to teach, only because there is more pressing need of getting to know *what* to teach. Of what weak avail it is that a teacher should know all the devices to be followed in composition work, if she uses bad English in her presentation, and is a bungler when it comes doing herself what she asks her pupils to do. The most skilful questions are spoiled if they are put in bad grammar or inexpert language. Linguistic and literary proficiency is as much to be required in a teacher of English as artistic skill and cultivation are required in a teacher of Art. The teacher must be a craftsman.

When it is fully understood and realized, however, that the first essential of good teaching is an adequate knowledge of the subject taught, and (in the case of English) a feeling for it and a power over it, we may safely proceed to consider more curiously questions of method.

We use the word "method" here to imply orderly procedure in one's work, in its largest aspects as in its minute details. We have more than once laid stress upon the initial importance of planning one's work. Good, clear, large planning is indispensable; and the plans must be the teacher's own, reflecting her own insights, her own hold upon the subject, her personal preferences and outlook. In Literature she is forbidden to teach what she does not like.

Plans are essential even for the most inspired, just because they are inspired. Their inspiration must be under control; and it must be assisted and get its chance by being unhampered by any anxiety as to the purpose it is serving. Inspiration runs to waste if it is not wisely employed. It is a steed that needs hitching to a serviceable wagon. The plan is this wagon. Besides, the teacher who does not plan well ahead, bears a harassing daily burden of anxious, hand-to-month contriving. If she has settled well in advance *what* she shall do, — which is not a matter of inspiration, but of careful ingenuity, — she may then devote her attention to the problem of *how* to do it, — of how to utilize the unforeseen circumstances of the hour; how to use those unexpected allies, or thwart those unsuspected difficulties, which are always turning up. Here is the chance for daily inspiration: let the teacher be free to take it.

In adopting plans she will be unwise to repose upon text-book plans. Slavishly to follow them is better, to be sure, than to have none at all; but is poor policy. In the first place, no teacher will see eye to eye with the writer of the text-book; she must at least edit it for her own use, to play into the hands, not only of her own capacities and stock of knowledge, but also of the outfit and needs of her pupils. We recall here an instance which, although it did not occur in connection with elementary school work, is apt. A certain much-used text-book, treating of diction, proceeds in traditional fashion to insist upon the importance of purity, etc., and warns against barbarisms. The student (first year Secondary School) must restrain his weakness for using obsolete words, "ycleped, for called" ! he must shun hybrids, e.g., "singist" ! for singer, and resist the temptation to bandy such technical words as "anneal," "reagent." We heard this gravely recited by a first year Secondary School class. What teacher with sound sense, who plans with an eye for her own real boys and girls, will waste time in this way ? Who, in dealing with common errors, localisms, or slang, will not consider the actual barbarisms to which her own pupils are prone, instead of strange text-book importations ? Her own plans will provide closely and liberally for her own boys and girls with their actual outfit, their peculiar shortcomings, their actual circumstances, and their probable destiny; and will ignore the irrelevancies of the text-book, which is to be her servant and not her master.

But there are some special difficulties against which we must be on our guard. In teaching English, more especially in the earlier years, perspective and emphasis, suggestion and imitation, are so important and yet so elusive and fluid, that planning is as difficult as it is necessary. The chief difficulty may be indicated by the word *thoroughness;* to be thorough enough, and thorough with the kind of thoroughness possible in such a matter as language; to avoid pedantic, literal, murderous thoroughness — how difficult that is !

That would be an absurd thoroughness in drawing which would keep a child drawing circles until it could draw a perfect one. Similarly, it would be a choking pedantry in English work that would confine a child to the practice of certain words or forms of speech until its usage was rigorously perfect. Clearly, thoroughness in an art is a relative thing, — relative to the general powers of the child; it can only be approximate. But to allow so much is to open the door, it might seem, to slovenliness, to touch-and-go methods, to the fine haphazard, spontaneous, unpondered work which is done by some "inspired" teachers, — day-by-day, hand-to-mouth work. This is to run with blind scare from Scylla straight into the clutches of Charybdis. There must be a plan that, while recognizing the indeterminateness of the child's growth in the grasp and use of language, in appreciative and creative power, nevertheless aims at certain definite, restricted results, so far as these can be proximately secured from the child. The teacher must by experience form her expectations as to the degree of thoroughness that may be expected, and then work systematically and clearly for it step by step. In some few things absolute accuracy may be worked for, — as in memorizing work, in the pronunciation or enunciation of certain words, in the general form of the written work; but in most things (such as the meanings of words, spelling, handwriting, story-telling) we must be satisfied with that, by dint of good example, patient practice, wise correction, and frequent but changeful (and disguised) repetition, the child can on an average attain to.

As to method generally, it is nothing more than developed common sense, as Huxley insists somewhere.[1] One may be well versed in the theory of method and yet be a very poor teacher: for no method can be successful without the tact that comes of careful, cautious practice. However, one teacher's experience may assist others in developing a method of their own; and the writer therefore puts on record what he regards as the more important counsels of perfection which have formed themselves in his own mind, with the possibility of their being of use to some fellow workers :-

1. To teach one thing at a time, but always in relation to one's plan as a whole; as an outgrowth of what has gone before, and as pointing forward to what is to succeed. Figuratively, provide every fact with proper couplings, so that it may take its place in services. Beware of discursiveness and miscellaneousness.

2. To let everything attempted either by oneself or one's pupils be done as well as it can the first time, and not indifferently well because there will be a chance to improve upon it later, for

(a) As to the teacher's part, the first impression or impact upon the child is incalculably important, color-

---

1 Huxley's essay on Descartes' famous "Essay on Method" is worth many of the more technical treatments of this topic, and has the recommendation of being well and attractively written. De Garmo's "Essentials of Method" (Heath) will be found helpful.

ing all subsequent dealings with the matter: hence, it should be as clean and strong, as telling and unforgettable, as stimulating and suggestive, as it can be made; and

(b) As to the child, any initial slackness discounts subsequent effort. The child ceases to be "all there." We have in mind, as an evil in English work, the practice so often permitted of making first the "rough" copy of the composition, and then the "fair," improved copy. Sometimes this is unavoidable or desirable; but there ought to be as little of it as possible, as it begets children who can do nothing "out of hand," with promptness and certainty of attack. It fosters slovenliness and half-heartedness. In reading. similarly, the beginner must do his best at the first attempt.

3. While, however, the deep first impression is very important, it is not by any means sufficient in order to secure lasting interest in the deeper sense of that term, — the sort of interest that will brace the energies for any drudgery that it may be necessary to undertake; the sort of interest that is a motive toward the discipline of the will. And to fail to secure this sturdier kind of interest, is a very serious defeat in attempting to teach a subject like Literature, in which interest is the very breath of life. That the indispensable initial wave of interest may not spend itself to little and partial purpose, it must be backed by another which shall catch this, and sweep the new thing into vital relations with the existing interests of the child. In technical terms, it is not enough that the new thing should be perceived; it must be apperceived; must receive a warm welcome into the child's mental habitation, and open up communications and sympathetic alliances with the old dwellers in that habitation.

4. To insure this result it is desirable to prepare the way, or, to keep to our trope, to herald the approach of the newcomer; so that the child may sympathetically go out to meet it in a mood, and with knowledge enough, to stimulate appreciation. This means (1) creating a favourable attitude of mind and a right

emotional atmosphere, (2) removing obvious stumbling-blocks in the way of the child's approach to the subject, — any strange, puzzling facts that are prominent in the poem or story, unfamiliar names, allusions, a knowledge of which is vital.

5. To get in one's masses first is the phrase, borrowed from the studio, that best expresses our next counsel. Begin always with the large, salient aspects of things: ignore all detail that may be ignored, in order to get a powerful seizure of a thing as a whole. Fill in details later — and for the very young child, the fewer the better. How far to elaborate detail the teacher's tact must decide. Exhaustive treatment is always a mistake; the plant must be left growing in the mind.

6. *Repetitio mater studiorum:* this maxim of the Jesuit educators is peculiarly true of literary studies. One must be always deepening one's hold on the old and great things, lovingly recalling them and conning them, as we do with the great tunes and pictures. Repeat, review, *revive* continually; but in new and unexpected ways, in new lights, in altered perspective, in fresh connections. Some new effect is usually to be gained by comparison or contrast. Encourage delighted brooding, especially upon the big things that will stay with one; let the affections gather more and more massively about them.

7. To develop in the child a sense of responsibility toward his knowledge and powers. Make him a reverent curator of his treasures; call him continually to account. Above all, let him "do something about it'; i.e., turn his possessions to use. Hold him, however, to strict account only on work actually done with him, and on things he is expected to know — not on outside or supplementary matters.

8. Be as independent of your text-book as possible. Know well the literature you use. Have a full memory. Work out of your appreciation: *le caeur au métier.*

6

Summary—Ideals and Aims in the Teaching and Study of English, with some Criticisms of Prevailing Practices

IN conclusion we may attempt to summarize some of our leading points and to supplement these with a few after-thoughts.

I. Literature and Language must be taught from their own distinctive point of view, — the point of view of Art. They are not information studies; they are not sciences; they aim to develop, not knowledge, but power, — imaginative sympathy, sensibility, admiration. This means that when a teacher passes from a lesson in Geography, let us say, to one in Reading, her point of view must undergo a complete change. Now she has quite other aims than those pursued in her geography work; now the whole atmosphere of the class room has altered. She has been dealing in her geography work with facts and their logical connection; now she is dealing with the emotional interpretation of facts, with experience in its relation to human hopes and fears, fancies and imaginings, desires and duties, ideals and aspirations. The fact is now of less importance than the spiritual rendering or interpretation of it, the emotional response to it. Has she been telling the little people about the winds — breeze, gale, hurricane — and the points of the compass — polar North and tropic South ? Now she turns to poetry, and lo ! the wind has become a human presence for the child :-

"O you that are so strong and cold,
O blower, are you young or old ?
Are you a beast of field or tree,
Or just a big, strong child like me ?"

and by and by the naive imagination of the child, which conceives of the weird horseman riding by in the moaning darkness, will become the adult imagination which, with Shelley, feels the "wild west wind" as the very "breath of Autumn's being."[1]

What we too often find is that the teacher has not this fundamental perception of the meaning and function of Literature. Literary products are handled grossly, for their fact values; or, in the higher grades, as products the merely intellectual comprehension of which calls for certain explanations, grammatical or allusional. But what has to be worked for is spiritual discernment and emotional apprehension. This defect is not to be wondered at. To handle Literature as such requires not a little culture; and culture, in the form of aesthetic insight, is the last requirement we have made of our teachers. We speak out of experience as a teacher of teachers; and we assert that the teacher who knows what the specific and proper office of Literature is, as distinguished from that of Science, is a rare and precious exception; and rarer still is one who can distinguish a first class poem or short story form a second or third rate one, or can apply the fundamental canons of literary criticism.

Let us hasten to say that the teachers are not wholly, nor indeed principally, to blame in this matter. They are not always taught, nor are they always in their teaching expected, to deal with Literature as such. We have already cited an illustration of this from the Language Number of *New York Teachers' Monographs*. We pointed out that the examination questions on the "Lady of the Lake," which were put to the graduating classes

1. The difference between the scientific and the poetic statement of a fact is concretely and happily illustrated by Edmund Clarence Stedman in his "Elements of Poetry."

in public schools to secure admission to the Secondary Schools, included not a single literary question among the ten of them, but that the paper was a grammar paper almost entirely. What teacher can do good literary work with such a paralyzing test to prepare for? How can she prevent her term's work from being other man stupid drudgery and rude butchery, which must disgust her pupils with Literature altogether?

II. Passing from appreciation to usage, the fundamental principle to be followed is that the mastery of language is a matter of practice, — practice animated by interest and enthusiasm, guided by good models and by wise counsel and criticism. Children learn their native tongue by imitation; and imitation continues to be, throughout the school course, the chief factor in language work. The rules of Grammar and rhetorical precept are later and comparatively unimportant means to the end sought. Of models, the most influential is the teacher herself; the influence of book models is heavily discounted if the teacher's own practice is not exemplary and winning. And by example we mean, first and foremost, oral example. Here again we have been very slack in our requirements, very low in our standards. The shortcomings of the average teacher as a writer are serious enough (we speak after much reading of teachers' compositions, note-books, etc.). Their unguarded spoken language, however, is worse than their written productions. The standard to-day (thanks to the energetic efforts of such men as Superintendent William H. Maxwell) is rather higher, doubtless, than it was a few years ago when Dr. Rice reported the results of his observations; but it is still ridiculously low. One still hears at times bad grammar and idiom; while as for any stylistic quality, revealing literary or artistic feeling, how rare it is ! We also look in vain in the average school for good, cultivated pronunciation, clear enunciation, pleasant tones, a proper use of the vocal organs. Again we say, small blame as a rule to teachers, who neither by training nor examination are impressed with the importance of these things. And this brings us to our next point.

III. The basis of all literary training is oral. The ear is the arbiter of speech; the mouth, not the pen, its greatest instrument. Not "Does it look right ?" but "does it sound right ?" is the first and fundamental test of language; it is the ready test of everyday life, and the final test of the great poets and masters of Literature. We are more and more a reading and writing people, to be sure; and yet we must not undervalue the practical importance of oral proficiency as an element of success in life. To be "well spoken" is still a strong point in a man's favor in many walks of life. The pleasant voice and delivery, the breeding implied in correct speech, the evidence of character and culture in the touch of distinction in the vocabulary, the power of graphic description and narration, — these things have sometimes even a commercial value; while ability to read and recite agreeably, to debate and argue effectively, is almost everywhere a valuable asset, and in certain callings — political, ministerial, legal — an indispensable condition of success.

We must gain the ear of the child; that is at first our only resource as teachers; and our chief resources it ought to be at all times. We must cultivate the child's auditory taste as, in our art work, we must cultivate his visual taste. It is well-known that many of our errors in spelling are the outcome of faulty oral impression. But we do not act upon this theory. We address our language work in the main to the eye, and slight the art of the tongue. We do not examine orally either our pupils or our teachers. A teacher's habits of speech may be abominable, but we do not find it out; and we shall not, until we make much of oral examinations. Worse still, when we do discover it, we are not troubled by it. We have been inclined to greet as a fantastical heresy Professor Corson's proposal that our literary examinations shall be tests in reading; and that literary culture shall mean, first of all, vocal culture. But his arguments in his admirable little book, "the Aims of Literary Study" (to which we have already drawn the attention of teachers), are in the main irrefutable. We must follow Dr. Corson's line of argument, too, in maintaining that the greatest influences in the literary education of the child are those which flow from the impressive vocal rendering of great poems by the teacher. (A great poem ill presented is like a great picture seen in a poor light.) These may be made great character-forming experiences in the life of the child; great spiritual experiences. And the psychologists are with us in attaching importance to this neglected side of literary training. Mr. Tracy, in his "Psychology of Childhood' (Heath), quotes the French dictum, "*L'oreille est le chemin du coeur*" — "The ear is the pathway to the heart' — and adds, "there is no sense, in the education of which greater care should be taken than the sense of hearing."

We have been led almost insensibly from one aspect of vocal and auditory training (considered, i.e., as a means to correct, skilful, refined discourse) to the other (considered as the chief means of spiritual interpretation) as the pathway to the heart, as the means therefore of moral and spiritual education. This is a principal point, which takes us from the more technical to the largest cultural view of our subject. Hence the great importance we ought to attach to vocal accomplishment in the teacher — good reading and reciting and story-telling. A special plea should be made for good story-telling. The story, we think, ought to play a much more prominent part than it has played in the class room. Story-telling, with all the magic of personal coloring and mimicry in oral delivery, should be one of the teacher's best accomplishments. Story-telling — anecdote, the gleaning from experience and reading to entertain company, as the peasant balladist in the hut, the Arab in his tent, the gypsy by the wayside or around the camp-fire, makes use of it — may be a much more powerful agency in our education than we have made of it hitherto.

Nothing but good would come of the attempt to be less print-ridden, to forsake and forget, more than is our wont, the cold printed page, and to catch warmth and glamour from the voice. We shall stand no chance of getting this, however, until we demand from our teachers pleasant, pure, and flexible utterance; a feeling for rhythm and rhyme; a power of evoking the onomatopoetic, alliterative, and musical effects of language.

IV. The supreme aim of literary and linguistic training is the formation of character. This includes and transcends all other aims; and it is because it is an aim which can be more effectually realized by Literature and Language that by any other study, that Literature, by almost common consent, must hold the central and dominating place in our school curriculum. The springs of a man's character are in his loves and hates, his tastes and desires, his ideals and aspirations; and the life of these depends much upon the light and the perspective with which they have been invested by the imagination. This imaginative exaltation of life, of noble human longings and ideals, it is the province of art, and especially of Literature as the highest art, to achieve, and, in turn, to foster and communicate. Here we have the starting- point and the goal of all education, and the master-motive of all literary discipline and nurture. We do not educate primarily for knowledge; for the possession of knowledge affords no guarantee that it will be worthily employed. It is a means to an end; and that end is the animating interest, the controlling aim and impulse, of a man's activity. We communicate knowledge in vain if we do not evoke stable and growing interests and enthusiasms. Of what avail all our nature study, if it has not quickened a love of nature, an ennobling curiosity and reverent wonder in the presence of the physical world ? Of what avail our history study, if it is not a treasured Ariadne's thread to lead us through the labyrinth of the problems, personal, social, and political, that wall us about on all sides ? Of what avail to have read Shakespeare and Milton, Emerson and Lowell, if the intercourse has not provoked a life-long thirst for helpful and inspiring communion with them and other great spirits ? If by our clumsiness we have killed or lessened the love of Letters in any child, we have made a curse of the literary knowledge we have given him.

And yet the love which it is the supreme purpose of Literature to generate or deepen in the child, is not love of literary culture itself, but rather of the life which Literature reflects and irradiates. "We create life through ideals," said Pestalozzi; and it is to bring the child under the sway of noble ideals of manhood and womanhood, noble types of life, noble deeds, noble feelings and thoughts about life and the duties and opportunities of living, — for this that Literature must be employed. To read great books with one's heart and imagination in the reading, is, in a certain sense, to live; to gain vicarious experience. And this life, in which we participate through books, — because it is invested with an imaginative halo, and has an ideal suggestiveness, completeness, and force, which provoke admiration and longing, — is so important because it sets up imitative tendencies that carry us into action. We all tend to become what we admire; to copy the men and women to whom we have given our hearts away. It is through these, as embodying ideals that have hypnotized us and have spread a subtle, sweetly tyrannizing influence through our being, that we are creating our own life and shaping our destiny, to recur to Pestalozzi's thought.

Here, then, in so using Literature as to form character, is the teacher's most important and delicate task. To accomplish it, she must know how to deal with Literature vitally as a form of life, as a means of embodying and creating ideals that cast their imaginative spell about the child. She must herself have lived vitally and must have related her culture to her living, to her quest for ideals, to her own deepest experiences. Only life begets life; only what comes from the heart goes to the heart; and it is only as the teacher has herself first drawn life from Literature that she can communicate its life to others. "The most valuable critic," says Dowden, "is the critic who communicates sympathy by an exquisite record of his own delights." The words may be applied to the teacher; her own delight in what she is reading or teaching must be as a fountain of life in a dry place. Her own likes may be ignored in teaching other subjects; but here the absence of liking cannot be pardoned. For the twentieth time, it may be, she has to teach her little class, "Piping down the valleys wild"; for the twentieth time she feels and communicates the joy of that beautiful lyric. For the twentieth time she has to repeat with older pupils, "Yet once more, O ye laurels," and the old thrill is hers once more. As well might she think of remaining insensitive to the fiftieth return of spring, or the daily pageant of sunset and the starsprent heavens, as of remaining unmoved by these miracles of the poet's art.

There is one pitfall, however, that awaits those who are eager in the pursuit of this final aim, — that of forcing the didactic note. A work of art is not a sermon or a pulpit; and we wrong it when we compel it to argue, or use it to enforce our own little moralizing text. Art recognizes that the syllogism is less powerful than the parable in its effect upon character; that a man's arguments are not so expressive as his personality and habits. It seems necessary to insist upon this, because teachers and textbooks have a noticeable leaning to what is "preachy" in Poetry and Literature; they tend to treat Literature as they would the Ten Commandments. That is the result of failure to apprehend the true nature of Literature as a form of art; to recognize that its influence is silent and subtle, reaching the reason through the emotions; affecting profoundly and unconsciously the child's moods and temper; his way of looking at, and feeling about, things. That is why full justice must be done to the beauty of Literature, even in the interests of its moral effect. We must not neglect its sensuous appeal; the color and singing quality of its words; its cadences and rhythms.

V. The development of appreciative power is the best of aids in the development of expressional power. In other words, expression is intimately related to impression. The best class in Composition is generally the best class in Literature. Those can give most and best who have received most and best. Children learn to write as they learn to swim, — by watching and imitating others; by trying under the lead of a model. They develop a feeling and instinct and knack for writing, without which they will never be effective as writers. Unless one can develop this craftsmanlike pride and interest one labors to small results. The child or youth who writes well is he who feels that he has something to say, wants to say it, and to say it well — to make his point. He naturally falls back, consciously or unconsciously, upon examples known to him. A workmanlike regard for this tools, a sense of responsibility toward the medium in which he is working, — this is what we want in the end to develop; and this is developed, not by rule and injunction, but by catching the spirit and developing the conscience of the craft through the persistent effort to practice it.

It is a great and very common mistake to dissociate the two sides, the appreciative and the creative; to neglect to use the one as a main agency in the development of the other. A professor who has written a text-book on composition is reported as having said at an educational conference: "It seems really axiomatic that in school work the study of English Literature is less necessary than the study of what makes correct, everyday English." This position is weak, on every score, we believe; whether from the point of view of culture, or of character development, or of expressive power; but it is unfortunate chiefly because it sets up a sort of rivalry between two complementary studies and interests. Our composition work ought to be much more imitative than it is: much more resonant with echoes of the work of the masters; but it will but be until we make much more extensive use of models than we have done. Mr. Webster, in his recent book on Composition (Houghton, Mifflin & Co.), so full of good counsel and suggestion, has gone so far as to adapt his Secondary School Course in Literature to serve the ends of his Course in Composition. This is dangerous, we think; because literary study has its own independent ends to serve. There is less danger in reversing the order. The experience of most of us, I venture to say, tallies with that of the college examiner, who found that of boys from two schools, those who came from the school where much zestful reading was done, excelled those who came from the one where, with less attention to Literature, a "thorough" drill in Composition and Rhetoric was given. The sense of form, which is the vital matter, had been better developed in the successful boys by the influence of models, than in others by the rigor of rule.

Needless to say that what applies to the taught, applies to the teacher; she also, as a craftsman, must draw inspiration and power from the great masters; she must live in the atmosphere of the great literary accomplishments of the race; must consult and study perpetually masterpieces of the class which she is trying to get her pupils to produce, and must keep alive by practice her own creative powers. Let her work with her children as the master-workman of eld worked with his apprentices, — as an exemplar as well as a preceptor.

VI. One common fault in our present practice is due to the failure to see that thought and language are twin products, and that we must deal with both in order to deal effectively with either. We speak, e.g., of working for a vocabulary, without recognizing that the accumulation of a vocabulary implies growth of thought, the development of cognition. "The growth of mind," as Professor Laurie says "and the growth of language in the mind go together. There has to be organized in the boy the language of his inner life, so that the language may grow with the life, and the life with the language." This development of the inner life can be no more effectively aided than by the endeavour to express it in language. Such a personal view of the case we fail to take. The new college entrance requirements illustrate this failure. They, and the examination papers based upon them, are in nothing so defective (excepting only the omission of oral tests) as in their composition tests, which are confined to subjects drawn from the books prescribed for reading and study. Such tests do not throw a student back upon himself; and they give the false impression that Composition has to do with reproducing (which often is nothing else than *re*- organizing) the material drawn from books and from class instruction. The kind of Composition which life, and even college work, will require from the student, will be of no such stilted, academic character. The man will have to express *himself*, his own interests, experience, knowledge. This disregard of the personal equation explains why composition work in our Grammar and our Secondary

Schools is often so very poor, so lifeless, so artificial, so impersonal, so bookish. Here is the bane of the Reproduction, which figures so largely in our work: the student eels that he is merely asked to do over again what is done already in his books. This is well-enough, if the aim is to test knowledge and its orderly storage in the mind: a student will see the point of that; but he instinctively feels that, for a test of his ability to compose, he must have the fresh, challenging task of delving in the field of his own mental possessions, selecting the pertinent ones, sorting and arranging them for the first time, and giving them an attractive form and that interesting personal quality which they will have only if he is really true to himself. Here it is not so much *what* he knows — the less he is troubled about that the better; it is *how* he knows it, and can tell it, to impress and interest others. His principal problem is one of organization.

VII. Self-expression is natural to the child; it is a form of self-activity in which he delights, provided we touch his real interests, or wisely tax his ingenuity. But as a rule his composition work is a bore and a "grind," as he calls it. That is our fault; partly because we are thinking in routine, text-book terms of the task, and of getting the child to do justice to it, instead of thinking of the child, and of getting him to do justice to himself; partly also because we do not set the child free from anxiety as to *what* he shall say, and allow him to put all his strength upon the way of saying what he has at easy command. Not that he has not to be tried by any discipline. In this, as in all other work, he has to learn how to take pains, to conceive and carry out a plan, to stick to his work until it is completed, and to toil on after the first impulse has failed him.

VIII. A danger to which we are liable, under the stress of our new ideals and enthusiasms, is over-ambition, or perhaps reckless ambition. Quantity menaces quality, and precocity (which is usually to be deplored) threatens us. We have made a plea (see Chapter III) for education according to Plato's conception of it, as appropriate and sufficient nurture or feeding; and we feel strongly that our English work, especially, may be much more nutritious (which does not mean more advanced) than it has been. But we do not nourish if we either overfeed or misdeed or overtax, and our ambitious new programmes show a tendency toward all these things. If we attempt too much at once, we do nothing thoroughly; and we get into confusion, slovenliness, and forgetfulness. Our work may be simple and yet rich, instead of being like much work in the past, simple and starving; as white flour is simpler than brown, but less feeding. To illustrate, — Wordsworth's "We are Seven," Blake"s "Little lamb, who made thee ?" are no less simple than Isaac Watts's preceptive rhymes; but they make twice as much brain-stuff. They are suggestive; and so they take root and grow, if properly seeded down. To do little work, so it be of the telling kind, rather than much of an indifferent quality; and to do this little cleanly, finely, so that it sticks, — this is what we want. And this is even more true of work in Composition than in Literature: we must be careful not to ask for too much, recognizing that a child's receptive and appreciative powers outrun his expressive powers, and that time must be allowed for the digestion of what he receives.

IX. We must avoid waste in order to get good results; and this we shall do when (1) our programmes are more organic and unified than they are now, and (2) when the work of each grade is done by the teacher in the light of the course as a whole, and according to the final ends aimed at.

(1) Our English Course ought to show a definite organizing policy animating and articulating the work of each and every grade; a network of connecting tissue uniting it all. The work of each grade must be clearly defined and well-developed; advancing steadily from the point where the work was left in the preceding grade, and covering just as much new ground as can be covered on the road toward the goals fixed by the course. In general (we are too well-aware of exceptional circumstances) each teacher ought to be able to rely, in English work, as confidently as she may in such obviously step-by-step studies as Arithmetic, upon certain definite accomplishment and conquests in the class that comes up to her at the beginning of the year —

no less and no more. Such and such specific bad habits ("ain't" and 'saw'r") have been attacked in preceding grades; certain powers (the comprehension of what a paragraph means, and of how to construct two related paragraphs in a simple scheme of contrast) have been exercised; such and such poems and stories have been read, re-read, memorized, used for comparative purposes, etc. These powers will now be re-exercised in the advance toward new difficulties; and the class will at the end of the year carry a very definitely enlarged inheritance to the next grade — no less and no more. The teacher, on such a plan, much learn to leave certain mistakes and failings alone, although they may chafe her. They will be struggled with in a later grade. Let her, in her reading, press her development work and her explanations only up to the fixed limits; in her written work, attempt only such and such forms of composition. Limitation will be the condition of effectiveness.

(2) The success of such a plan must depend upon the teacher's ability to see the work of her grade in its organic relation, not only to the work of the grade below and the grade above her own, but as a stage in the progress toward certain final results, and as a contribution to those results. Not only does it give interest and meaning to her work thus to foresee the bud in the seed, the full flower in the bud, the fruit in the flower; but it is the necessary condition of unity of aim and continuity of development in the school work. No elementary teacher can do her work effectively who is not working upon the same general principles, grammatical, rhetorical, and critical, as those upon which the Secondary School or College teacher is working. She must, therefore, have a good theoretical and practical command of those principles. She is simply applying them at a different stage of the child's development, and needs a peculiarly delicate skill, born of a divination of the child's nature, in order so to apply them. She must bring something of the same high critical standards to her choice and treatment of literature; something of the same feeling for style as the Secondary School or

College teacher should bring. She, too, is working, in ways appropriate to the age of her pupils (now empirically, now rationally, now synthetically, now analytically), for Clearness. Force and Rhythm, for Purity and Propriety, for Coherence and Sequence; and she must know accurately and fully both what these qualities are, and the chief secrets of their attainment.

So recurs once more the refrain to our various criticisms — the need of a higher literary culture among our teachers, higher standards, better and richer training. Here we have the first condition of any noteworthy improvement in our school work. It is unnecessary to pass any detailed criticism upon the English teaching in our Normal Schools and Training Colleges; it is, on the average, admittedly inadequate. We do not lose sight of the fact that English is only one of many subjects which the Elementary School teacher is called upon to teach; but we affirm that it is the most important subject, the core and the foundation of the curriculum, disciplining the mind to truer, wider vision, purifying and deepening the emotions that are the main factors in character, bracing and strengthening the will to the patient control and the energetic and noble use of the powers of heart and mind.

Our plea for English culture, broad and deep, as the one thing needful in our teachers of English, is made in no partisan or exclusive spirit. We are not of those who are in any way jealous of the claims and assertiveness of Science. Our ideal in education is not a distinctively literary education; and to us anything like a literary pose, literary snobbery or pretentiousness, is utterly intolerable. It is a wholesome experience for a literary man to have to serve his time in a technical school, where the students are all for Science and the Crafts, and regard Literature and Language as species of refined, purgatorial requirements. He works without a halo: no shy, illusive light lends enchantment to his devotions to the Muses. He must win respect for his subject by its blood-red, purple-veined humanism; by its sheer power over the heart; by its resistlessly attractive dealings with recognizable real, palpitating things. No fine flutings, no dainty work-devices, will avail. And this, we say, is wholesome for both teacher and taught. Would there were more of such frankly human testing of literary products, to exterminate the brood of triflers who are the victims of that graphomania which we have had diagnosed for us of late. No; let us have, as the best basis for literary appreciation and effectiveness, a sturdy love and zest of life, a feeling for the glory and greatness and sacredness of it, the common human and natural quality of it; — for this great round earth, so strangely afloat among the constellations; these restless millions upon it — heroes and nobles, conquerors and conquered; this tragic-comic drama of human life, and the great inheritances which Science and Art have left us, and which need no literary advertising. Above all let us prize a first-hand knowledge of Duty and Love, Courage and Honor, Justice and Freedom: happy are we if we can get or evoke these as foundations for that glorification of them which Literature achieves.

We need not fear to set the highest humanitarian standards for ourselves. Our danger is less that of unduly magnifying our teaching office than of dropping to the level of a commonplace professionalism. We should come nearer being priests than purveyors; and indeed, it is in the growth of the feeling that is beginning to pervade our ranks of our being a lay priesthood, called to the cure of young souls, that we have cause for highest hope. This is true of all teachers, whatever their subject; for there is none but has its ethical, its religious serviceableness. But to the teacher of Literature this view applies in the most obvious way. His best and ultimate aim must be to help his pupils to partake in an exceptional degree, through the greatest works in Poetry, of the highest fruits of the ethical and religious consciousness of man; — to effect through them that cleansing, that purgation, which was regarded by the master-mind of antiquity as the high religious office of its greatest literary products, its Drama. To instill ideals, through contact with them in Literature; to promote self-command and worthy self-expression through the cultivation of power over the tongue, — such is the calling to which the teacher of English is properly self-dedicated.

Sketch of Secondary School course in English literature, showing how the work may be massed to secure both coherence and progression while varied to include the leading literary species

Kind of Work	First Year	Second Year	Third Year	Fourth Year
1	2	3	4	5
	Emphasis at the start on narrative species. Scott's narrative poems.	*Beginning with emphasis on descriptive species.*	*Beginning with emphasis on expository species.*	*Emphasis on argumentative species.*
Epic and Ballad	"Soharb and Rustum." Homer (Ulysses in Phæacia). Ballads, ancient and modern; short and long.	"Ancient Mariner," "Forsaken Merman."	"Idylls of the King."	
Lyric, Idyllic and Reflective		Gray's "Elegy," Goldsmith's "Deserted Village," Byron's "Childe Harold," etc. Keats's "Eve of St. Agnes," etc.	Dryden : Odes, Epistles, "Palamon and Arcite." Prose. Pope : Epistles; "Essay on Criticism"; "Rape of the Lock."	
Shakespeare	"Julius Cæsar," [Plutarch, Froude.]	"Merchant of Venice."	"As You Like It," "Midsummer Night's Dream."	"Macbeth." [Comparative Study of Drama.]

Contd.

1	2	3	4	5
Milton		"L'Allegro," and "Il Penseroso."	Sonnets and some prose.	"Comus" and "Lycidas."
Short Story and Novel	Hawthorne, Poe, Irving, Kipling, Bunner, Stockton, etc. "Ivanhoe" etc.	"Silas Marner," "Christmas Carol," "Lorna Doone," "Cloister and the Hearth," etc.	"Vicar of Wakefield," "Cranford," Pride and Prejudice," "Esmond," Dickens, etc.	["Romola," "House of the Seven Gables," etc.]
Miscellaneous Prose : Essay, Sketch, Biography, etc.	Life and Letters of Hawthorne and Scott.	"Travels with a Donkey," etc. Burroughs (for Nature interest), etc.	Bacon, Milton, Bible. Swift, Defoe, Bunyan, De Coverley Papers, Macaulay's Addison.	Macaulay's Milton (with Mark Pattison's or Raleigh's biographies). Carlyle's "Essay on Burns."
Speeches and Orations	Lincoln's Gettysburg Speech	Curtis: "Public Duty of Educated Men."	Webster.	Burke (Morley's Life).

The arrangement does not indicate the order in which the works should be taken in any year. See text, Chap. 1.

Only a few books, among the many from which choice might be make, have been named; and these, for the sake of suggestion. for additions see the List of Books for Home Reading Recommended by the Conference on College Entrance Requirements in English. The most flagrant omissions are American poets and writers (Emerson, Lowell, Holmes), and such great names as Shelley, Wordsworth, and Browning; De Quincey, Landor, and Ruskin. These may be substituted for those authors who have already been read in the Grammar Grades, or may be introduced for comparative or collateral reading.

7

Education

THEREFORE, first teach — as I have said in the preface to *Unto This Last* — "The Laws of health, and exercises enjoined by them" ; and, to this end, your schools must be in the fresh country and amidst fresh air, and have great extents of land attached to them. Riding, running, all the honest, personal exercise of offence and defence, and music, should be the primal heads of this bodily education.

Next to these bodily accomplishments, the two great mental graces should be taught, Reverence and Compassion: not that these are in literal sense to be "taught," for they are innate in every well-born human creature, but they have to be developed exactly as the strength of the body must be, by deliberate and constant exercise. I never understood why Goethe says that reverence is not innate, but must be taught from without; it seems to me so fixedly a function of the human spirit, that if men can get nothing else to reverence they will worship a man, or an idol, or a vegetable.

But to teach reverence rightly is to attach it to the right persons and things; first, by setting over your youth masters whom they cannot but love and respect; next, by gathering for them, out of past history, whatever has been most worthy in human deeds and human passion; and leading them continually to dwell upon such instances; and lastly, by letting them justly feel, as far as may be, the smallness of their own powers and knowledge, as compared with the attainments of others.

Compassion, on the other hand, is to be taught chiefly by making it a point of honour, along with courage, and in the same rank (as it is indeed the complement and evidence of courage), so that, in the code of unwritten school law, it shall be held as shameful to have done a cruel thing as a cowardly one. All infliction of pain on weaker creatures is to be condemned as unmanly crime; and every possible opportunity taken to exercise the youths in offices of some practical help, and to acquaint them with the realities of the distress which, in their youthful enthusiasm for the joys of life, it is so difficult for those who have not seen suffering at home to conceive.

Reverence then and compassion, we are to teach primarily, and with these, as the bond and guardian of them, truth of spirit and word of thought and sight. Truth, earnest and passionate, sought for like a treasure, and kept like a crown.

This teaching of truth as a habit will be the chief work the master has to do; and it will enter into all parts of education. First, you must accustom the children to close accuracy of statement; this both as a principle of honour, and as an accomplishment of language, making them try always who shall speak truest, both as regards the fact he has to relate or express (not concealing or exaggerating), and as regards the precision of the words he expresses it in, thus making truth (which, indeed, it is) the test of perfect language, and giving the intensity of a moral purpose to the study and art of words: Then carrying this accuracy into all habits of thought and observation also, so as always the *think* of things as they truly are, and to *see* them as they really are, as far as in us rests. And it does rest much in our power, for all false thoughts and seeings come mainly of our thinking of what we have no business with, and looking for things we want to see, instead of things that ought to be seen.

"Do not talk but of what you know; do not think but of what you have materials to think justly upon; and do not look for things only that you like, when there are others to be seen"- this is the lesson to be taught to our youth, and inbred in them; and that mainly by our own example and self-control. Never teach a child anything of which you are not yourself sure; and, above all, if you feel anxious to force anything into its mind in tender years, that the virtue of youth and early association may fasten it there, be sure it is no lie which you thus sanctify. There is always more to be taught of absolute, incontrovertible knowledge, open to its capacity, than any child can learn; there is no need to teach it anything doubtful. Better that it should be ignorant of a thousand truths, than have consecrated in its heart a single lie.

And for this, as well as for many other reasons, the principal subjects of education, after history, ought to be natural science and mathematics; but with respect to these studies, your schools will require to be divided into three groups: one for children who will probably have to live in cities, one for those who will live in the country, and one for those who will live at sea; the schools for these last, of course, being always placed on the coast. And for children whose life is to be in cities, the subjects of study should be, as far as their disposition will allow of it, mathematics and the arts; for children who are to live in the country, natural history of birds, insects, and plants, together with agriculture taught practically; and for children who are to be seamen, physical geography, astronomy, and the natural history of sea fish and sea birds.

JOHN RUSKIN, *Time and Tide.*

The chief vices of education have arisen from the one great fallacy of supposing that noble language is a communicable trick of grammar and accent, instead of simply the careful expression of right thought. All the virtues of language are, in their roots, moral; it becomes accurate if the speaker desires to be true; clear, if he speaks with sympathy and a desire to be intelligible; powerful, if he has earnestness; pleasant, if he has sense of rhythm and order. There are no other virtues of language producible by art than these: but let me mark more deeply for an instant the significance of one of them. Language, I said, is only clear when it is sympathetic. You can, in truth, understand a man's word only by understanding his temper. Your own word is also like an unknown tongue to him unless he understands yours. And it is this which makes the art of language, if any one is to be chosen separately from the rest, that which is fittest for the instrument of a gentleman's education.

To teach the meaning of a word thoroughly, is to teach the nature of the spirit that coined it; the secret of language is the secret of sympathy, and its full charm is possible only to the gentle. And thus beautiful speech is always the outcome of sincere and kindly speech. False speech, apparently beautiful, may be constructed on principles imitated from those out of which sincere and truly beautiful speech has arisen; but all such utterance, whether in oration or poetry, is not only without permanent power, but it is destructive of the principles of sincerity it has usurped. So long as no words are uttered but in faithfulness, so long the art of language goes on exalting itself; but the moment it is shaped on external principles, it falls into frivolity, and perishes.

And this truth would have been long ago manifest, had it not been that at certain periods there is always a tendency to deny the sincerity of the first masters of language. Once learn to write gracefully in the manner of an ancient author, and we are apt to think that he also wrote in the manner of someone else. But no noble nor right style was ever yet founded but out of a sincere heart.

No man is worth reading to form your style, who does not mean what he says; nor what any great style ever invented but by some man who meant what he said. Find out the beginner of a great manner of writing, and you have also found the declarer of some true facts or sincere passions; and your whole method of reading will thus be quickened, for, being sure that your author really meant what he said, you will be much more careful to ascertain what it is that he means.

And of yet greater importance is it deeply to know that every beauty possessed by the language of a nation is significant of the innermost laws of its being. Keep the temper of the people stern and manly; make their associations grave, courteous, and for worthy objects; occupy them in just deeds; and their tongue must needs be a grand one. Nor is it possible, therefore, that any tongue should be a noble one, of which the words are not so many trumpet-calls to action. All great languages invariably utter great things, and command them; they cannot be mimicked but by obedience; the breath of them is inspiration because it is not only vocal, but vital; and you can only learn to speak as these men spoke, by becoming what these men were.

JOHN RUSKIN, *Lectures on Art.*

John Ruskin (1819-1900) is one of the great teachers of art and life to the modern world. He held that no nation which is not truly healthy and great can produce great art, and he was, therefore, impelled to stray from his special subject, that of art criticism, to propound his conception of a liberal education and a sound sociology. The first passage is from *Time and Tide*, a series of letters to an English working man in 1867, when the extension of the franchise in England had concentrated his attention on the importance of sound views on education for the new voters. The second passage is from *Lectures on Art* delivered by Ruskin in 1870 as professor of fine art at the University of Oxford. *Unto this Last*, 1862, consists of four papers, originally contributed to the *Cornhill Magazine.*

p. 1, 1. 6. ***personal exercises of offence and defence.*** All those healthy exercises in which a man is engaged either in defending his body or attacking an opponent. Ruskin is probably mainly thinking of boxing and fencing, but the words might equally apply to most out-door games.

p. 1, 1. 16. ***Goethe says that reverence is not innate.*** In *Wilhelm Meister's Travels*, chap. x.

p. 1, 1. 17. ***it seems to me so fixedly a function of the human spirit.*** To regard some person or thing with awe seems to be one of the deepest instincts in man, to belong to his very nature.

p. 2, 1. 20 ***Reverence then and compassion . . . like a crown.*** It is important for the young to be taught reverence and sympathy for others; but they will be unable a retain these unless they can also be taught to be sincere in their principles (truth of spirit) and in the words they speak, to set a value upon thinking clearly, and seeing things as they actually are (truth of sight). Truth should be sought for seriously and with the whole heart and soul, and when discovered should be preserved as the most valuable of all a man's possessions. A crown = the symbol of royal power, the most coveted of all worldly honours

p. 2, 1. 29. ***as an accomplishment of language.*** It is not easy to express exactly what you mean in words; it can only be done after you have acquired considerable mastery over the language and a wide knowledge of the use of words.

p. 3, 1. 3. ***giving the intensity of a moral purpose to the study and art of words.*** They should be taught to regard the study of words and skill in their use with the same respect as they regard good conduct.

p. 3, 1. 22. ***be sure it is no lie which you thus sanctify.*** The child believes readily and without suspicion what you tell it. An idea which enters a child's mind and is connected with its earliest experience of the world remains more firmly fixed there than later ideas — the idea become as it were sacred, believed in with the strongest faith (the word "consecrated" later in the passage is used in the same sense). The teacher should beware therefore not to impart false notions to the child in these early years.

p. 4, 1. 17. ***a communicable trick of grammar and accent.*** It has been commonly supposed, quite erroneously that a teacher can impart to a pupil the power of expressing his thoughts in stately and impressive language merely by making him proficient in the grammar of the language and teaching him correct pronunciation.

p. 4, 1. 18. ***all the virtues ....moral.*** Language whether spoken or written can only possess good qualities if the speaker or writer himself possesses those qualities. Examples of these are given in the second part of the sentence.

p. 4, 1. 24. ***producible by art.*** Art by itself is incapable of adding any other good qualities to those enumerated above

p. 4, 1. 29. ***temper*** = temperament.

p. 5, 1. 3. ***To teach the meaning.......gentle.*** If you wish your pupils to understand the full meaning of a word you must show them the circumstances under which it first came into use, and the sense in which it was first used. Thus the word "spirit" in this passage originally meant "breath" and it various subsequent senses are all derived from that. Only one who has a real appreciation of the full meaning of words can use them effectively.

p. 5, 1. 19 ***at certain periods.........masters of language.*** During periods when there are few original writers, and good writing is supposed to consist in imitating the style and manner of the great writers of earlier times, people come to believe that these great writers themselves imitated the language of others and did not express their own thoughts in their own special way.

p. 5, 1. 32. ***will thus be quickened.*** Lit. "be made to live" — so "will have a real value or purpose for you."

p. 6, 1. 5. ***every beauty.......laws of its being.*** Every beautiful word or manner of expression in a language is an indication of a corresponding virtue in the character of the nation that speaks it. Examples of these follow.

p. 6, 1. 12. ***trumpet-calls to action.*** If the language is a noble one it will inspire the speakers of it to noble deeds, because the words themselves suggest noble feelings and ideals.

p. 6, 1. 14. ***command them*** — bring them into existence.

p. 6, 1. 14. ***they cannot be mimicked........vital.*** You cannot reproduce really great language by merely imitation noble passages; your language will be great if you really feel and possess (are obedient to) the high ideals which inspired it. Great language is inspiring not only because it is high sounding but because it actually communicates lofty thoughts and ideals.

8

The Character of a Gentleman

HENCE it is that it is almost a definition of gentleman to say that he is one who never inflicts pain. This description is both noble and, as far as it goes, accurate. He is mainly occupied in merely removing the obstacles which hinder the free and unembarrassed action of those about him; and he concurs with their movements rather than takes the initiative himself. His benefits may be considered as parallel to what are called comforts or conveniences in arrangements of a personal nature; like an easy chair or a good fire, which do their part in dispelling cold and fatigue, though nature provides both means of rest and animal heat without them.

The true gentleman in like manner carefully avoids whatever may cause a jar or a jolt in the minds of those with whom he associates; — all clashing of opinion, or collision of feeling, all restraint, or suspicion, or gloom, or resentment; his great concern being to make everyone at their ease and at home. He has his eyes on all his company; he is tender towards the bashful, gentle towards the distant, and merciful towards the absurd; he can recollect to whom he is speaking; he guards against unseasonable allusions, or topics which may irritate; he is seldom prominent in conversation, and never wearisome. He makes light of favours while he does them, and seems to be receiving when he is conferring. He never speaks of himself except when compelled, never defends himself by a mere retort, he has no ears for slander or gossip, is unwilling to impute motives to those who interfere with him, and interprets everything for the best. He is never mean or little in his disputes, never takes unfair advantage, never mistakes personalities or sharp sayings for arguments, or insinuates evil, which he dare not say out.

From a far-seeing prudence, he observes the maxim of the ancient sage, that we should ever conduct ourselves towards our enemy as if he were one day to be our friend. He has too much good sense to be affronted at insults, he is too well-employed to remember injuries, and too tolerant to bear malice.

He is patient, forbearing, and resigned, on philosophical principles; he submits to pain, because it is inevitable, to bereavement, because it is irreparable, and to death, because it is his destiny. If he engages in controversy of any kind, his disciplined intellect preserves him from the blundering discourtesy of better, perhaps, but less educated minds; who, like blunt weapons, tear and hack instead of cutting clean, who mistake the point in argument, waste their strength on trifles, misconceive their adversary, and leave the question more involved than they find it.

He may be right or wrong in his opinion, but be is too clear- headed to be unjust; he is as simple as he is forcible, and as brief as he is decisive. Nowhere shall we find greater candour, consideration, indulgence; he throws himself into the minds of his opponents, he accounts for their mistakes. He knows the weakness of human reason as well as its strength its province and its limits.

If he be an unbeliever, he will be too profound and large-minded to ridicule religion or to act against it he is too wise to be a dogmatist or fanatic in his infidelity. He respects piety and devotion; he even supports institutions as venerable, beautiful, or useful to which he does not assent; he honours the minister of religion, and it contents him to reject its mysteries without assailing or denouncing them. He is a friend of religious toleration, and that, not only because his philosophy has taught him to look on all forms or faith with an impartial eye, but also from the gentleness and tenderness of feeling, which is the attendant on civilization. J. H. NEWMAN, *Idea of a University*

John Henry Newman (1801—1890) was the foremost religious writer and preacher of his century. Originally an Anglican clergyman, he was received into the Catholic Church in 1845, and towards the close of a long life he was created Cardinal. Newman had a rare power of expressing himself, his ideal position and spiritual experiences sincerely, clearly and exactly. His famous delineation of a "gentleman" is a faithful presentment of himself, and especially of his own bearing to opponents in the controversies into which he was drawn in defence of his new Church.

p. 10, 1. 4. ***removing the obstacles......himself.*** The chief concern of the gentleman is simply to put all who come in contact with him at their ease, everything they do he accepts a natural and proper, he does not attempt to set them right or impose his own thoughts or manners on them.

p. 10, 1. 21. ***distant*** = people who are reserved, who do not readily form an intimacy.

p. 10, 1. 22. ***merciful towards the absurd.*** He shows a kindly disposition towards those who behave in a ridiculous fashion, he refrains from making them conscious of their absurd behaviour.

p. 10, 1. 23. ***unseasonable allusions.*** He is careful not to refer to matters which may cause pain or annoyance to those present.

p. 11, 1. 9. ***little*** = small minded, mean spirited.

p. 11, 1. 10. ***never mistakes personalities...arguments.*** He never makes the mistake of supposing that a contemptuous remark aimed at one's opponent or a harsh or biting remark helps an argument.

p. 11, 1. 19. ***on philosophical principles.*** The study of philosophy is supposed to produce a calm and serene temperament. So here, his naturally calm temperament leads him to be patient, etc.

p. 11, 1. 23 ***his disciplined intellect....educated minds.*** He has all his faculties under complete control : so in argument he never makes the mistake of being rude or abrupt; people who do this may be cleverer than he intellectually, but they show thereby that they are less cultured.

p. 11, 1. 31. ***he is as simple.....decisive.*** The arguments he uses may be simple but they are convincing, they may be short but they settle the question.

p. 12, 1. 2. ***he throws......opponents.*** He has imagination: i.e., he can put himself into the mind of his opponent and understand why he holds certain opinions he does.

p. 12, 1. 5. ***its province.*** He knows when and on what subjects the reasoning faculty of man can be brought into operation with profit.

p. 12, 1. 17. ***attendant on civilization*** = It is the product of civilization. Civilization refines the feelings.

9

A Poet's Estimate of His Poetry

COLEORTON,

May 21, 1807

My Dear Lady Beaumont,

Though I am to see you so soon, I cannot but write a word or two, to thank you for the interest you take in my poems, as evinced by your anxiety about their immediate reception. I write partly to thank you for this, and to express the pleasure it has given me, and partly to remove any uneasiness from your mind which the disappointments you sometimes meet with, in this labour of love, may occasion. I see that you have many battles of fight for me — more than, in the ardour and confidence of your pure and elevated mind, you had ever thought of being summoned to; but be assured that this opposition is nothing more than what I distinctly foresaw that you and my other friends would have to encounter. I say this, not to give myself credit for an eye of prophecy, but to allay any vexatious thoughts on my account which this opposition may have produced in you.

It is impossible that nay expectations can be lower than mine concerning the immediate effect of my little book upon what is called the public. I do not here take into consideration the envy and malevolence, and all the bad passions which always stand in the way of a work of any merit from a living poet; but merely think of the pure, absolute, honest ignorance in which all worldlings of every rank and situation must be enveloped, with respect to the thoughts, feelings and images on which the life of my poems depends. The things which I have taken, whether from within or without, what have they to do with dinners, morning calls, hurry from door to door, from street to street, on foot or in carriage; with Mr. Pitt or Mr. Fox or with political elections? In a word what have they to do with the endless talking about things nobody cares anything for except as far as their own vanity is concerned? What have they to do (to say all at once) with a life without love? In such a life there can be not thought, for we have no thought (save thoughts of pain) but as far as we have love and admiration.

It is an awful truth, that there neither is, nor can be, any genuine enjoyment of poetry among nineteen out of twenty of those persons who live, or wish to live, in the broad light of the world—among those who either are, or are striving to make themselves, people of consideration in society. This is a truth, and an awful one, because to be incapable of a feeling for poetry, in my sense of the word, is to be without love of human nature and reverence for God.

Upon this I shall insist elsewhere; at present let me confine myself to my object; which is to make you, my dear friend, as easy-hearted as myself with respect to these poems. Trouble not yourself upon their present reception; of what moment is that compared with what I trust is their destiny? To console the afflicted; to add sunshine to daylight, by making the happy happier; to teach the young and the gracious of every age to see, to think, and feel, and therefore, to become more actively and securely virtuous; this is their office, which I trust they will faithfully perform, long after we (that is, all that is mortal of us) are mouldered in our graves. I am well aware how far it would seem to many I overrate my own exertions, when I speak in this way, in direct connection with the volume I have just make public.

I am not, however, afraid of such censure, insignificant as probably the majority of those poems would appear to very respectable persons. I do not mean London wits and witlings, but grave, kindly-natured, worthy persons, who would be pleased if they could. I hope that these volumes are not without some recommendations, even for readers of this class : but their imagination has slept; and the voice which is the voice of my poetry, without imagination, cannot be heard....

My letter (as this second sheet, which I am obliged to take, admonishes me) is growing to an enormous length; and yet, except that I have expressed my calm confidence that these poems will live, I have said nothing which has a particular application to the object of it, which was to remove all disquiet from your mind on account of the condemnation they may at present incur from that portion of my contemporaries who are called the public.

I am sure, my dear Lady Beaumont, if you attach any importance to it, it can only be from an apprehension that it may affect me, upon which I have already set you at ease; or from a fear that this present blame is ominous of their future or final destiny. If this be the case, your tenderness for me betrays you.

Be assured that the decision of these persons has nothing to do with the question; they are altogether incompetent judges. These people, in the senseless hurry of their idle lives, do not read books, they merely snatch a glance at them, that they may talk about them. And even if this were not so, never forget what, I believe, was observed to you by Coleridge, that every great and original writer, in proportion as he is great or original, must himself create the taste by which he is to be relished; he must teach the art by which he is to be seen; this, in a certain degree, even to all persons, however wise and pure may be their lives, and however unvitiated their taste. But for those who dip into books in order to give an opinion of them, or talk about them to take up an opinion—for this multitude of unhappy, and misguided, and misguiding beings, an entire regeneration must be produced; and if this be possible, it must be a work of time.

To conclude, my ears are stone-dead to this idle buzz, and my flesh as insensible as iron to these poetry stings; and, after what I have said, I am sure yours will be the same. I doubt not that you will share with me an invincible confidence that my writings (and among them these little poems) will co-operate with the benign tendencies in human nature and society, wherever found; and that they will, in their degree, be efficacious in making men wiser, better and happier. Farewell ! I will not apologize for this letter, though its length demands and apology. Believe me, eagerly wishing for the happy day when I shall see you and Sir George here.

Most affectionately yours,

W. WORDSWORTH.

Introduction. Sir George Beaumont and his wife were close friends of the poet ***William Wordsworth*** (1770-1850). During the years 1806-07 Wordsworth was staying at a farm-house at Coleorton in Leicestershire, lent to him by Sir George Beaumont, whose house and grounds were close by. The little book referred to in the letter was published in 1807 and contained, among other poems, *The Happy Warrior.* Wordsworth's early publications were very coldly received by the public, who were accustomed to the artificial style of poetry which had been popular in England for 150 years, and did not understand either Wordsworth's ideas or his new and apparently uncouth style. Nevertheless the poet was confident, as he explains in this letter, that ultimately their merits would be recognized. This passage is especially valuable as explaining how poetry influences men, and the value of that influence.

p. 14, 1. 18. ***eye of prophecy.*** The ability to see into the future.

p. 15, 1. 1. ***what is called the public.*** Wordsworth means here the reading public. Only sympathetic readers who took the trouble to understand his aims were likely to be pleased with his poetry. Besides, he desired and hoped that his poetry might eventually be read and appreciated by peasants and the lower classes, who would not in his time be considered as part of the reading public.

p. 15, 1. 5. ***honest ignorance.*** Genuine ignorance, in contrast with the pretended ignorance of spiteful critics, who purposely misconstrue the poet's meaning.

p. 15, l. 9. ***The things which I have taken....political elections.*** How can people engaged in the busy affairs of the world, in society or politics, for example, appreciate the subjects presented in my poems ? ***From within or without*** = thoughts and feelings of the poet, and the images and scenes which he describes.

Mr. Pitt. William Pitt had actually died on 23rd of January, 1806, but he here represents the Tory party. Charles James *Fox,* his chief opponent, a Whig, was a member of the Coalition Government which was in power when this letter was written.

p. 15, l. 17. ***a life without love***—a selfish, self-seeking life. Wordsworth imagined that politicians and men of the world were for the most part heartless.

p. 16, l. 6. ***gracious.*** People of a kindly and courteous disposition.

p. 16, l. 7. ***securely virtuous.*** Wordsworth in this fine passage admirably explains the purpose and value of poetry. By refining the feelings and making men more sensitive to beauty and truth it influences their conduct which in its turn becomes refined (virtuous), and all fear that their instincts may lead them astray disappears. They acquire a sense of security as to their conduct.

p. 16, l. 17. ***London wits and witlings.*** The cultured society of London, including the fashionable writers and critics. A wit = a person generally belonging to fashionable society who was noted for his clever conversation and power of repartee.

p. 16, l. 17. ***grave, kindly-natured, worthy persons.*** Probably Wordsworth here refers to such people as Lord Jeffrey (1773-1850), who severely criticized his poetry in the *Edinburgh Review,* not out of malice but simply because he preferred inferior poetry of the eighteenth-century kind and did not understand the new spirit in Wordsworth's poetry.

p. 16, l. 21. ***imagination***= (1) the creative power of the mind, such as the poet displays when in his poetry he produces *new* thoughts or images, e.g., Hamlet is the creation of Shakespeare's imagination; (2) similar power which exists in a greater or less degree in all minds, which when active enables them to appreciate the creations of men of genius—this is the sense in this passage. Cf. also II, note, p. 12, 1. 2.

p. 17, 1. 5. ***ominous***=foreshadowing disaster or ill-fortune.

p. 17, 1. 6. ***betrays you***=leads you to make a mistake.

p. 17, 1. 13. ***Coleridge*** (1772-1834) was a common friend of the Beaumonts and of Wordsworth. He was a philosopher, critic and poet.

p. 17, 1. 15. ***must himself create the ......relished.*** A writer who introduces a new style or new thought, as every great writer does, cannot hope to be understood or appreciated at once, he must first show people how to appreciate him (create the taste).

p. 17, 1. 19. ***unvitiated***—uncorrupted, unspoiled—so refined.

p. 17, 1. 21. ***to take up.*** A rather unusual sense=to criticise, almost to contradict—they talk about a book merely to attack someone else's opinion about it.

p. 17, 1. 23. ***regeneration***=a change of heart or attitude.

10

A Poet's Influence on John Stuart Mill

THIS state of my thoughts and feelings made the fact of my reading Wordsworth for the first time (in the autumn of 1828) an important event of my life. I took up the collection of his poems from curiosity, with no expectation of mental relief from it, though I had before resorted to poetry with that hope. In the worst period of my depression, I had read through the whole of Byron (then new to me), to try whether a poet, whose peculiar department was supposed to be that of the intenser feelings, could rouse any feeling in me. As might be expected I got no good from this reading, but the reverse. The poet's state of mind was too like my own. His was the lament of a man who had worn out all pleasures, and who seemed to think that life, to all who possess the good things of it, must necessarily be the vapid, uninteresting thing which I found it. His Harold and Manfred had the same burden on them which I had : and I was not in a frame of mind to desire any comfort from the vehement passion of his Giaours or the sullenness of his Laras. But while Byron was exactly what did not suit my condition, Wordsworth was exactly what did. I had looked into the "Excursion" two or three years before, and found little in it; and I should probably have found as little, had I read it at this time. But the miscellaneous poems, in the two-volume edition of 1815 (to which little of value was added in the latter part of the author's life), proved to be the precise thing for my mental wants at that particular juncture.

In the first place, these poems appealed powerfully to one of my strongest feelings, the love of rural objects and natural scenery; to which I had been indebted not only for much of the pleasure of my life, but quite recently for relief from one of my longest relapses into depression. In this power of rural beauty over me, there was foundation laid for taking pleasure in Wordsworth's poetry; the more so, as his scenery lies mostly among mountains, which, owing to my early Pyrenean excursion, were my ideal of natural beauty.

But Wordsworth would never have had any great effect on me, if he had merely placed before me beautiful pictures of natural scenery. Scott does this still better than Wordsworth, and a very second-rate landscape does it more effectually than any poet. What made Wordsworth's poems a medicine for my state of mind, was that they expressed, not mere outward beauty, but states of feeling, and of thought coloured by feeling, under the excitement of beauty. They seemed to produce that very culture of the feelings, which I was in quest of. In them I seemed to draw from a source of inward joy, of sympathetic and imaginative pleasure, which could be shared in by all human beings; which had no connection with struggle or imperfection, but would be made richer by every improvement in the physical or social condition of mankind. From them I seemed to learn what would be the perennial sources of happiness, when all the greater evils of life shall have been removed. And I felt myself at once better and happier as I came under their influence.

There have certainly been, even in our own age, greater poets than Wordsworth; but poetry of deeper and loftier feeling could not have done for me at that time what his did. I needed to be made to feel that there was real, permanent happiness in tranquil contemplation. Wordsworth taught me this, not only without turning away from, but with a greatly increased interest in, the common feelings and common destiny of human beings.

And the delight which these poems gave me, proved that with culture of this sort, there was nothing to dread from the most confirmed habit of analysis. At the conclusion of the Poems came the famous Ode, "Intimations of Immortality" : in which along with more than his usual sweetness of melody and rhythm, and along with the two passages of grand imagery so often quoted, I found that he too had similar experience to mine; that he also had felt that the first freshness of youthful enjoyment of life was not lasting ; but that he had sought for compensation, and found it, in the way in which he was now teaching me to find it.

The result was that I gradually, but completely, emerged from my habitual depression, and was never again subject to it. I long continued to value Wordsworth less according to his intrinsic merits, than by the measure of what he had done for me. Compared with the greatest poets, he may be said to be the poet of unpoetical natures, possessed of quiet and contemplative tastes. But unpoetical natures are precisely those which require poetic cultivation. This cultivation Wordsworth is much more fitted to give, than poets who are intrinsically far more poets than he.

It so fell out that the merits of Wordsworth were the occasion of my first public declaration of my new way of thinking, and separation from those of habitual companions who had not undergone a similar change. The person with whom at that time I was most in the habit of comparing notes was Roebuck and I induced him to read Wordsworth, in whom he also at first seemed to find much to admire : but I, like most Wordsworthians, threw myself into strong antagonism to Byron, whose writings he regarded as the poetry of human life, while Wordsworth's, according to him, was that of flowers and butterflies.

We agreed to have the fight out at our Debating Society, where we accordingly discussed for two evenings the comparative merits of Byron and Wordsworth, propounding and illustrating by long recitations our respective theories of poetry.

This was the first debate on any weighty subject in which Roebuck and I had been on opposite sides. The gulf between us widened for this time more and more, though we continued for some years longer to be companions. In the beginning, our chief divergence related to the cultivation of the feelings. Roebuck was a lover of poetry and of most of the fine arts. He took great pleasure in music, in dramatic performances, especially in painting, and himself drew landscapes with great facility and beauty. But he never could be made to see that these things have any value as aids in the formation of character.

He saw little good in any cultivation of the feelings, and none at all in cultivating them through the imagination. It was in vain I urged on him that the imaginative emotion which an idea, when vividly conceived, excites in us, is not an illusion but a fact, as real as any other of the qualities of objects and is quite consistent with the most accurate knowledge and most perfect practical recognition of all its physical and intellectual laws and relations. The intensest feeling of the beauty of a cloud lighted by the setting sun, is no hindrance to me knowing that the cloud is vapour of water, subject to all the laws of vapours in a state of suspension; and I am just as likely to allow for, and act on, these physical laws whenever there is occasion to do so, as if I had been incapable of perceiving any distinction between beauty and ugliness.

JOHN STUART MILL, *Autobiography.*

This passage from the autobiography of ***John Stuart Mill*** (1806-1873) is interesting, first, as showing the growing popularity which Wordsworth confidently predicted for his poetry (cf. III, p. 16, 1. 3), and, secondly, as showing the reasons of that popularity. He was appreciated for his intense love of nature and his beautiful presentation of it : for his gravity, sincerity, his deep interest in "the spiritual side of common life," his exalted philosophical thought (as in the Ode mentioned below), and also for his strong, pure and usually simple style. Wordsworth's belief that nature could not only become a source of joy and comfort to man, but was also capable of refining the feelings and so also the conduct, attracted men like Mill who were engaged in purely speculative studies. It became a kind of religion with them.

p. 21, 1. 8. ***Byron.*** George Gordon, Lord Byron (1788-1824), was the most popular writer in England during his lifetime. Some of his chief works are referred to here—*Child Harold's Pilgrimage* (Harold) in four cantos, published 1812-1817 ; *Manfred, a poetical drama, 1817 ; and the two romances Lara,* 1814 and *The Giaour*, 1813.

p. 21, 1. 9. ***whose peculiar department........interser feelings.*** His popularity was due to the highly emotional manner in which he treated his subjects : but his manner, especially that of the earlier romances, which was often flashy and insincere, has now largely lost its charm as it did for Mill.

p. 21, 1. 12. ***The poet's state of mind.*** The feeling of melancholy and dissatisfaction with life which pervades much of his earlier poetry.

p. 21, 1. 16. ***vapid.*** Flat, dull.

p. 21, 1. 18. ***burden.*** They showed that the poet was oppressed by the same melancholy feelings as Mill was.

p. 21, 1. 23. ***The "Excursion"*** —1814. A long poem by Wordsworth, discursive and dull in parts but containing a number of fine passages descriptive of nature or revealing Wordsworth's beliefs and attitude to life.

p. 22, 1. 7. ***juncture.*** The time when Mill's mind was in the state he had described, i.e., oppressed with dissatisfaction.

p. 22, 1. 17. ***my early Pyrenean excursion.*** Mill spent his fourteenth year in France. During this period he acquired a taste for French manners and thought which remained with him through life.

p. 22, 1. 17. ***my ideal.*** The word "ideal" is here used in its familiar sense = "answering to one's highest conception." Mountains were for Mill the highest form of natural beauty. But the word "ideal" is used especially by philosophers in the sense of the perfect type of anything, as in "the ideal state." Such a state can exist only in the imagination.

p. 22, 1. 21. ***Scott, Sir Walter*** (1771 - 1832). He frequently describes natural scenery both in his poems and in the *Waverley Novels.*

p. 22, 1. 22. ***a very second-rate landscape......any poet.*** Mill means that even a poor picture of a landscape gives a man a bitter idea of what the scene is like, because it is seen with the eyes, than any description by a poet. This statement is questionable, though it is partialy true of uncultured people.

p. 22, 1. 26. ***states of feeling........under the excitement of beauty.*** A true poet like Wordsworth does not merely describe beautiful scenes or beautiful objects but the feelings or the thoughts which beautiful objects produce in him. Poetry is always produced as the result of an excitement of the feelings, generally called emotion.

p. 22, 1. 30. ***a source of inward joy....... imaginative pleasure.*** The poems seemed to be able to create joy in me, to have the power of imparting through the imagination a similar pleasure to that which the poet evidently experienced in writing them. For the imagination cf. III., p. 16. 1. 21, note.

p. 23, 1. 5. ***shall have.*** According to the proper sequence of tenses the verb should be "had," by using "shall have" Mill indicates his belief that the greater evils of life will one day be removed. The removal is not conditional but a fact.

p. 23, 1. 12. ***tranquil contemplation.*** Wordsworth believed that man could obtain happiness, contentment and peace of mind through the calm contemplation of nature.

p. 23, 1. 15. ***common feelings.......human beings.*** The characters depicted in Wordsworth's poems are drawn from humble life, the feelings and emotions described are those in which every man can share. From reading his poems a man is likely to find an increased interest in the lot and circumstances of mankind.

p. 23, 1. 18. ***nothing to dread.....analysis.*** A good deal of MIll's work, his Study of Logic, for example, demanded critical examination of his material. People always engaged in analysing, whether it be substances or ideas, are apt to lose their appreciation of these things as wholes, as well as of the beauty in nature. They "murder to dissect," as Wordsworth says. Mills feels that Wordsworth's poetry will counteract this danger.

p. 23, 1. 20. ***famous Ode.*** The full title of *Ode on Immations of Immortality from Recollections of Early Childhood*, published in 1807.

p. 23, 1. 23. ***two passages.*** These are probably stanza "Our birth is but a sleep and a forgetting," and stanza "Thou whose exterior semblance doth belie."

p. 24, 1. 1. ***intrinsic.*** Belonging properly to him as poet, that is, his poetic qualities.

p. 24. 1. 3. ***Poet of unpoetical natures.*** He appeals people who are not naturally given to emotion, whose imagination is not readily moved.

p. 24, 1. 15. ***Roebuck.*** Born in Madras 1810 ; like his friend Mill he entered Parliament as a Radical, and maintains a position of independence from party ties throughout his political career.

p. 24, 1. 20. ***the poetry of human life........flowers and butterflies.*** The more forcible representation of human passions and feelings in Byron seemed to him to represent human life more truly than Wordsworth did. He failed to understand the really strong human sympathy in his work, which seemed only to consist in descriptions of such natural objects as birds and butterflies. Actually Byron's interest in life is much narrow than Wordsworth's, and is confined to the Society in which he moved.

p. 25, 1. 6. ***aids in the formation of character.*** For the influence of poetry on conduct cf. note to III., p. 16, 1. 6. all fine art has a refining effect upon the feelings.

p. 25, 1. 7. ***He saw little good.......beauty and ugliness.*** The idea expressed in this passage is that the cultivation of the sense of beauty which comes through an appreciation of the fine arts, poetry, for example, is as important for a truly cultured man as the acquiring of scientific knowledge. A feeling or beauty does not hamper scientific knowledge. In fact a sense of the beauty of nature helps towards a more perfect conception of it.

A NATURALIST IN THE FORESTS OF PARA

On leaving the town we walked along a straight suburban road constructed above the level of the surrounding land. It had low swampy ground on each side, built upon, however, and containing several spacious country houses, which were embowered in magnificent foliage. Leaving the last of these, we arrived at a part where the lofty forest towered up like a wall five or six yards from the edge of the path to the height of, probably, a hundred feet. The tree trunks were only seen partially here and there, nearly the whole frontage from ground to summit being covered with a diversified drapery of creeping plants all of the most vivid shades of green; scarcely a flower to be seen, except in some places a solitary scarlet passion-flower set in the green mantle like a star.

The low ground on the borders between the forest wall and the road was encumbered with a tangled mass of bushy and shrubby vegetation, amongst which prickly mimosas were very numerous, covering the other bushes in the same way as brambles do in England. Other dwarf mimosas trailed along the ground close to the edge of the road, shrinking at the slightest touch of the feet as we passed by. Cassia trees, with their elegant pinnate foliage and conspicuous yellow flowers, formed a great proportion of the lower trees, and arborescent arums grew in groups around the swampy hollows.

Over the whole fluttered a larger number of brilliantly coloured butterflies than we had yet seen ; some wholly orange or yellow, others with excessively elongated wings, sailing horizontally through the air, coloured black, and varied with blue, red, and yellow. One magnificent grassy-green species especially attracted our attention. Besides butterflies, there were few other insects except dragonflies, which were in great numbers.

After stopping repeatedly to examine and admire, we at length walked onward. The road then ascended slightly, and the soil and vegetation became suddenly altered in character. The shrubs here were grasses, low sedges and other plants, smaller in foliage than those growing in moist grounds. The forest was second growth, low, consisting of trees which had the general aspect of laurels and other evergreens in our gardens at home : the leaves glossy and dark green.

The sun, now, for we had loitered long on the road, was exceedingly powerful. The day was most brilliant; the sky without a cloud. In fact, it was one of those glorious days which announce the commencement of the dry season. The radiation of heat from the sandy ground was visible by the quivering motion of the air above it. We saw or heard no mammals or birds; a few cattle belonging to an estate down a shady lane were congregated, panting, under a cluster of wide-spreading trees. The very soil was hot to our feet, and we hastened onward to the shade of the forest which we could see not far ahead.

At length, on entering it, what a relief ! We found ourselves in a moderately broad pathway or alley where the branches of the trees crossed overhead and produced a delightful shade. The woods were at first recent growth, dense, and utterly impenetrable the ground, instead of being clothed with grass and shrubs as in the woods of Europe, was everywhere carpeted with fern-shaped mosses.

Gradually the scene became changed. We descended slightly from an elevated, dry, and sandy area to a low and swampy one ; a cool air breathed on our faces, and a mouldy smell of rotting vegetation greeted us. The trees were now taller, the under wood less dense, and we could obtain glimpses into the wilderness on all sides. The leafy crowns of the trees, scarcely two of which could be seen together of the same kind, were now far away above us, in another world as it were. We could only see at times, where there was a break above, the tracery of the foliage against the clear blue sky.

Sometmies the leaves were palmate, or of the shape of large outstretched hands; at others finely cut or feathery, like the leaves of Mimosas. Below, the trees trunks were everywhere linked together by the woody flexible stems of climbing and creeping trees whose foliage is far away above, mingled with that of the taller independent trees. Some were twisted in strands like cables, others had thick stems contorted in every variety of shape, entwining snake-like round the tree trunks, or forming gigantic loops and coils among the larger branches; others, again, were of zigzag shape, or indented like the steps of a staircase, sweeping from the ground to a giddy height.

Further on the ground became more swampy, and we had some difficulty in picking our way. The wild banana here began to appear, and, as it grew in masses, imparted a new aspect to the scene. The leaves of this beautiful plant are like broad sword-blades, eight feet in length and a foot broad; they rise straight upwards, alternately, from the top of a stem five or six feet high. Numerous kinds of plants with leaves similar in shape to these but smaller clothed the ground. The trunks of the trees were clothed with climbing ferns, and plants with large, fleshy, heart-shaped leaves. Bamboos and other tall grass and reed-like plants arched over the pathway.

The appearance of this part of the forest was strange in the extreme; description can convey no adequate idea of it. The reader who has visited Botanical Gardens may form some notion by conceiving a vegetation like that in the great palm-house spread over a large tract of swampy ground, but he must fancy it mingled with large trees covered with creepers and parasites, and figure to himself the ground encumbered with fallen and rotting trunks, branches, and leaves; the whole illumination by a glowing vertical sun, and reeking with moisture.

We often read, in books of travels, of the silence and gloom of the Brazilian forests. They are realities, and the impression deepens on a longer acquaintance. The few sounds of birds are of that pensive or mysterious character which intensifies the feeling of solitude rather than imparts a sense of life and cheerfulness. Sometimes, in the midst of the stillness, sudden yell or scream will startle one; this come from some defenseless fruit-eating animal, which is pounced upon by a tiger-cat or stealthy boa-constrictor. Morning and evening the howling monkey make a most fearful and harrowing noise, under which it is difficult to keep up one's buoyancy of spirit. The feeling of inhospitable wildness which the forest is calculated to inspire, is increased tenfold under this fearful uproar. Often, even in the still hours of mid-day, a sudden crash will be heard resounding afar through the wilderness, as some great bough or entire tree falls to the ground.

There are, besides, many sounds which it is impossible to account for. I found the natives generally are much at a loss in this respect as myself. Sometimes a sound is heard like the clang of an iron bar against a hard, hollow tree, or a piercing cry rends the air, these are not repeated, and the succeeding silence tends to heighten the unpleasant impression which they make on the mind.

With the native it is always the *Curupira,* the wild man or spirit of the forest, which produces all noise they are unable to explain. For myths are the rude theories which mankind, in the infancy of knowledge invent to explain natural phenomena. The *Curupira* is a mysterious being, whose attributes are uncertain for they vary according to locality. Sometimes he described as a kind of orang-otang, being covered with long, shaggy hair, and living in trees. At other he is said to have cloven feet, and a bright red face. He has a wife and children, and sometimes comes down to steal the mandioca.

At one time I had a Brazilian boy in my service, whose head was full of the legends and superstitions of the country. He always went with me into the forest ; in fact, I could not get him to go alone, and whenever we heard any of the strange noises mentioned above, he used to tremble with fear. He would crouch down behind me, and beg of me to turn back ; his alarm ceasing only after he had made a charm to protect us from the *Curupira.* For this purpose he took a young palm leaf, plaited it, and formed it into a ring, which he hung to a branch on our track.

H. W. BATES, *The Naturalist on the Amazons.*

H. W. Bates (1825 — 1892), naturalist and explorer. During eleven years' work on the banks of the Amazon in South America he collected 8000 species of insects new to science. *The Naturalist on the Amazons* (1863) was written at the urgent request of Charles Darwin, who considered Bates almost without a rival in describing a tropical forest.

p. 30, 1. 12. ***drapery.*** The trees which lined the road on either side were covered with different creepers from top to bottom, which hung from every branch like curtains.

p. 30, 1. 15. ***passion-flower.*** The name given to a number of creeping plants, one or two of which are to be found in gardens in India.

p. 30, 1. 20. ***mimosas.*** A family of plants and trees, of which the *babul* is one. The Sensitive plant is another ; this is the dwarf mimosa referred to two lines now.

p. 30, 1. 21. ***brambles.*** The bramble or blackberry bush is a thick prickly shrub to be found wild all over the British Isles.

p. 31, 1. 1. ***Cassia trees.*** The Indian *amaltas* is a species of Cassia.

p. 31, 1. 2. ***pinnate foliage.*** Having feather-shaped leaves.

p. 31, 1. 4. ***arborescent arums.*** Arums having a tree-like growth. The arum is known in Northern India as *ghanyan.*

p. 31, 1. 19 ***sedges.*** Kinds of grass-like plants growing in marshy ground or beside rivers.

p. 31, 1. 19. ***other plants, smaller in foliage*.....**different plants grow in different soils—damp marshy soil produces plants luxuriant in growth, as drier soil is reached the plants and trees become smaller and less luxuriant, of "second growth." Anyone who passes from the Taria to the Himalayas will notice this.

p. 31, 1. 22. ***laurels.*** A glossy-leaved shrub growing in Europe and temperate climates.

p. 31, 1. 28. ***radiation of heat.*** The ground becomes heated by the sun, and then itself emits rays of heat, which accounts for the quivering motion of the air which can be noticed on any hot dry day.

p. 32, 1. 11. ***fern-shaped mosses.*** A moss is a small green plant without flowers which may be seen growing on damp walls in India. These described here were a larger variety resembling a fern.

p. 32, 1. 17. ***we could obtain glimpses into the wilderness.*** Between the trunks of the trees could be seen the barren country surrounding the forest which they had just entered.

p. 32, 1. 22. ***tracery.*** The light from above penetrating between the leaves and branches gave the latter the appearance of carved stonework *(jāte).*

p. 32, 1. 24. ***palmate.*** Shaped like those of a palm.

p. 32, 1. 28. ***climbing and creeping trees*........**large creepers with stems as thick as those of trees—such as may be seen in any Indian forest.

p. 33, 1. 4. ***giddy height.*** To such a height that it made one dizzy to look at it.

p. 33, 1. 15. ***fleshy.*** Thick and full of pulp.

p. 33, 1. 22. ***the great palm-house.*** Such as is to be seen in most botanical gardens in India.

p. 33, 1. 25. ***parasites.*** Plants which obtain their nutriment from other plants or trees. The *amal bel* is a well-known parasite in Northern India.

p. 34, 1. 1. ***intensifies the feeling of solitude.*** The sounds are so few that when they are heard the silence which precedes and follows them only makes the solitude appear greater.

p. 34, 1. 8. ***horrowing noise......spirit.*** Harrowing = literally tearing, wounding, and so causing dread or depression to the spirits, making it difficult to remain cheerful.

p. 34, 1. 26. ***For myths.......natural phenomena.*** Savage or uncivilized peoples invent stories (myths) to explain anything which occurs in nature which they are unable to explain.

p. 34, 1. 29. ***attributes.*** Qualities, characteristics.

p. 34, 1. 31. ***orang-otang.*** A large long-armed man-like ape which is found in the islands of Borneo and Sumatra.

p. 35, 1. 3 ***mandioca.*** A root from which the inhabitants of Brazil make a kind of flour.

11

The Foundations of Scientific Knowledge

I CANNOT but think that the foundations of all natural knowledge were laid when the reason of man first came face to face with the facts of Nature; when the savage first learned that the fingers of one hand are fewer than those of both; that it is shorter to cross a stream than to head it; that a stone stops where it is unless it is moved, and that it drops from the hand which lets it go; that light and heat come and go with the sun; that sticks burn away in a fire; that plants and animals grow and die; that if he struck his fellow savage a blow he would make him angry, and perhaps get a blow in return, while if he offered him a fruit he would please him, and perhaps receive a fish in exchange. When men had acquired this much knowledge, the outlines, rude though they were, of mathematics, of physics, of chemistry, of biology, of moral, economical, and political science, were sketched. Nor did the germ of religion fail when science begun to bud.

Thus it seems impossible to imagine but that the foundations of all knowledge—secular or sacred,—were laid when intelligence dawned, though the superstructure remained for long ages so slight and feeble as to be compatible with the existence of almost any general view respecting the mode of governance of the universe. No doubt, from the first, there were certain phenomena which, to the rudest mind, presented a constancy of occurrence, and suggested that a fixed order ruled, at any rate, among them. I doubt if the grossest of Fetish worshippers ever imagined that a stone must have a god within it to make it fall, or that a fruit had a god within it to make it taste sweet. With regard to such matters as these, it is hardly questionable that mankind from the first took strictly positive and scientific views.

But, with respect to all the less familiar occurrences which present themselves, uncultured man, no doubt, has always taken himself as the centre and measure of the world ; nor could he well avoid doing so. And finding that his apparently uncaused will has a powerful effect in giving rise to many occurrences, he naturally enough ascribed other and greater events to other and greater wills, and came to look upon the world and all that therein is, as the product of the wills of persons like himself, but stronger, and capable of being appeased or angered, as he himself might be soothed or irritated.

Through such conceptions of the plan and working of the universe all mankind have passed, or are passing. And we may now consider what has been the effect of the improvement of natural knowledge on the views of men who have reached this stage, and who have begun to cultivate natural knowledge with no desire but that of "increasing God's honour and bettering man's estate."

For example, what could seem wiser to an ancient people, than that they should learn the exact succession of the seasons, as warnings for their husbandmen; or the position of the stars, as guides to their rude navigators? But what has grown out of this search for natural knowledge of so merely useful a character? You all know the reply. Astronomy, — which of all sciences has filled men's minds with general ideas of a character most foreign to their daily experience, and has, more than any other, rendered it impossible for them to accept the beliefs of their fathers. Astronomy,—which tells them that this so vast and seemingly solid earth is but an atom among atoms, whirling no man knows whither, through illimitable space; which demonstrates that what we call the peaceful heaven above us, is but that space, filled by an infinitely subtle matter whose particles are seething and surging, like the waves of an angry sea ;

which opens up to us infinite regions where nothing is known, or ever seems to have been known, but matter and force, operating according to rigid rules; which leads us to contemplate phenomena the very nature of which demonstrates that they must have had a beginning, and that they must have an end, but the very nature of which also proves that the beginning was, to our conceptions of time, infinitely remote, and that the end is as immeasurably distant.

But it is not alone those who pursue astronomy who ask for bread and receive ideas. What more harmless than the attempt to lift and distribute water by pumping it; what more absolutely and grossly utilitarian? Yet out of pumps grew the discussions about Nature's abhorrence of a vacuum; and then it was discovered that Nature does not abhor a vacuum, but that air has weight; and that notion paved the way for the doctrine that all matter has weight, and that the force which produces weight is co-extensive with the universe,— in short, to the theory of universal gravitation : while learning how to handle gases led to the discovery of oxygen, and to modern chemistry, and to the notion of the indestructibility of matter.

Again, what simpler, or more absolutely practical, than the attempt to keep the axle of a wheel from heating when the wheel turns round very fast? How useful for carters and drivers of carriages to know something about this ; and how good it would be if any ingenious person would find out the cause of such phenomena. Such an ingenious person was Count Rumford ; and he and his successors have landed us in the theory of the persistence, or indestructibility, of energy. And in the infinitely minute, as in the infinitely great, the seekers after natural knowledge of the kinds called physical and chemical, have everywhere found a definite order and succession of events which seem never to be infringed.

And how has it fared with Medicine and Anatomy? Have the anatomist, the physiologist, or the physician, whose business it has been to devote themselves assiduously to that eminently practical and direct end, the alleviation of the sufferings of mankind,— have they been able to confine their vision more absolutely to the strictly useful? I fear they are the worst offenders of all. For if the astronomer has set before us the infinite magnitude of space, and the practical eternity of duration of the universe; if the physical and chemical philosophers have demonstrated the infinite minuteness of the constituent parts and the practical eternity of matter and of energy; and if both have alike proclaimed the universality of a definite and predicable order and succession of events, the workers in biology have not only accepted all these, but have added more startling theses of their own. For, as the astronomers discover the earth to be no centre of the universe, but an eccentric speck, so the naturalists find man to be no centre of the living world, but one amidst endless modifications of life ; and as the astronomer observes the mark of practically endless time set upon the arrangements of the solid system, so the student of life finds the records of ancient forms of existence peopling the world for ages, which, in relation to human experience, are infinite.

Such are a few of the new conceptions implanted in our minds by the improvement of natural knowledge. Men have acquired the ideas of the practically infinite extent of the universe and of its practical eternity; they are familiar with the conception that our earth is but an infinitesimal fragment of that part of the universe which can be seen; and that, nevertheless, its duration is, as compared with our standards of time, infinite. They have further acquired the idea that man is but one of innumerable forms of life now existing on the globe, and that the present existences are but the last of an immeasurable series of predecessors. Moreover, every step they have made in natural knowledge has tended to extend and fix in their minds the conception of a definite order of the universe—which is embodied in what are called, by an unhappy metaphor, the laws of Nature—and to narrow the range and loosen the force of men's belief in spontaneity or in changes other than such as arise, out of that definite order itself.

Whether these ideas are well or ill founded is not the question. No one can deny that they exist, and have been the inevitable outgrowth of the improvement of natural knowledge. And if so, it cannot be doubted that they are changing the form of men's most cherished and most important convictions.

T. H. HUXLEY, *Essays*.

Thomas Henry Huxley **(1825-95) was one of the greatest English scientists of nineteenth century.** Although it is improbable that men in the early stages of civilization acquired knowledge exactly in the way Huxley imagines, and although some of Huxley's views have been now superseded, the essay is still valuable as giving in simple and striking language the meaning of the scientific attitude, its origin, its growth and its value of mankind.

p. 38, 1. 6. ***to head it*** = to go round the head of—to go up the stream until it was so narrow that it could be crossed with ease.

p. 38, 1. 18. ***Nor did the germ.....bud.*** The beginnings of scientific knowledge did not prevent ideas on religion from growing also. Germ=lit. a rudimentary form of a plant or animal out of which the plant or animal develops.

p. 38, 1. 22. ***the superstructure*** = the conclusions which they draw about science and religion.

p. 39, 1. 1. ***compatible with*** = it was possible to hold these conclusions along with almost any view of the nature of God. As scientific knowledge increased, especially after the fifteenth century, and particularly during the eighteenth and nineteenth centuries, it had a deep influence upon men's attitude to religion.

p. 39, 1. 7. ***Fetish worshippers.*** Worshippers of inanimate objects supposed to be habited by spirits, or to possess magical powers.

p. 39, 1. 12. ***positive*** here = "practical"—"matter-of-fact".

p. 39, 1. 15. ***taken himself as the centre and measure of the world*** = man has always regarded things in the world in their relation to himself. He has never been interested in them except in so far as they had some connection with himself—and he has always measured their qualities and powers by comparison with his own.

p. 39, l. 17. ***uncaused will.*** This refers to the apparent fact that man's will is free and independent of any external cause.

p. 39, l. 28. ***natural knowledge.*** Knowledge of nature.

p. 39, l. 31. ***"increasing God's honour and bettering man's estate."*** A slight variation of a passage in Bacon's *Advancement of Learning,* I, v. 11 : "Knowledge......a rich store-house for the glory of the Creator, and the relief of man's estate."

p. 40, l. 9. ***most foreign to*** = "farthest removed from."

p. 40, l. 10. ***rendered it impossible.......their fathers.*** Huxley is thinking of such stories as that of the Creation related in the first chapter of Genesis : which was once believed to be literally true.

p. 40, l. 17. ***infinitely subtle matter........an angry sea.*** According to physicists all space is filled with an elastic fluid called ether, which, like other substances, is composed of tiny particles—in Huxley's day called atoms—which are in constant motion.

p. 40, l. 29. ***who ask for bread and receive ideas.*** An application of a passage in the New Testament, St. Luke xi. 11. "If a son shall ask bread of any of you that is a father, will he give him a stone?" Here it means that those who study astronomy are seeking knowledge which may be of some practical value, and instead receive general ideas about the nature of the universe.

p. 40, l. 32. ***out of pumps.....air has weight.*** In the early days of engineering it was observed that if a piston in contact with water in a common pump is raised, the water follows the piston up the pump. The usefulness of the pump depends on this fact. The fact was "explained" by the statement that "Nature abhors a vacuum" (i.e., a completely empty space). The explanation seemed sufficient for a time; but there remained the fact that Nature seemed to "abhor a vacuum" only up to a height of thirty feet or so; for no common pump could be constructed to raise water more than this height. The failure was ascribed at first to imperfections in the pump. But Torricelli, an Italian engineer, showed the real reason of the rising of the water under the piston to be the pressure of the air on the water surface outside the pump. This pressure is sufficient to support a column of water about thirty feet in height. If then, by means of the piston, we remove the pressure on the top of the water column inside the pump, the outside pressure will force the inside water up just enough to balance by its weight the outside air pressure; but no more. And this led directly to the conclusion that the pressure of the air on the water surface outside is due to the fact that air possesses weight.

p. 41, 1. 5. *the force which......co-extensive with the universe.* Why does a stone fall to the ground when it is not supported ? It took a very long time to answer so simple a question. One's first answer would probably be, "Because it has weight." It was Newton who first tried to explain why bodies possess weight ; and he did so by assuming that every body is attracted by the earth, the attraction being proportional to the amount of matter in the body. But he was immediately driven to the conclusion that it is not the earth alone which attracts; and that every body attracts every other body in the universe with a force depending upon the amounts of matter in the two bodies, and the distance between them. This is, in fact, Newton's law of gravitation. He verified it by showing that enabled him to account with great exactness for the observed motions of the moon and other heavenly bodies, which until the time had defied the power of mathematicians.

p. 41, 1. 9. ***The indestructibility of matter*** = the theory that the total amount of matter in the universe always remained the same, though it may undergo any number of transformations.

p. 41, 1. 16. ***Count Rumford*** = Sir Benjamin Thompson a (1753-1814), famous scientist, who was born in America and created Count Rumford by the Elector of Bavaria, whom minister of war he became.

p. 41, 1. 18. ***persistence, or indestructibility, of energy.*** = Energy means the power to do work. Bodies may possess energy either because of their motion (e.g., the rapidly moving flywheel of an engine); or in virtue of their position (e.g., raise weights may be used to put a flywheel in motion if we allow them to descend); or in virtue of their physical or chemical state (e.g., our food, in undergoing the chemical process of digestion supplies us with the power to do work). It is believed that the total amount of energy in the universe is constant. It may be transferred from one body to another, or it may be transferred into energy of an apparently different kind, but its total amount does not change.

p. 41, 1. 23. ***seem never to be infringed*** = as far as we know seem never to be interrupted.

p. 41, 1. 25. ***physiologist*** = a student or teacher of the science of the functions and phenomena of living things.

p. 42, 1. 1. ***practical eternity*** = the universe may be considered eternal in so far as our interests and our lives are concerned.

p. 42, 1. 3. ***the infinite minuteness of its constituent parts,*** *i.e.,* of the atoms and molecules referred to above.

p. 42, 1. 6. ***the universality of.......succession of event*** = they have shown that throughout the universe events follow one another in an order which is certain, and which can be shown to hold good in all cases.

p. 42, 1. 9. ***theses*** = propositions.

p. 42, 1. 11. ***an eccentric speck*** = the earth, instead of being the centre of the universe with its axis placed centrally, is now seen to be not only situated outside the centre, but to be as a mere speck of dust in comparison with the universe and its millions of worlds.

p. 42, 1. 12. ***one amidst endless modifications of life*** = all life (both plants and animals) is continually undergoing modifications. Man as he now is the product of a series of such modifications through a process of evolution, and this process is still going on.

p. 42, 1. 16. ***the records of ancient forms......are infinite.*** Remains of ancient forms of animals and plants now no longer existing are found in rocks and are called fossils. The earliest of these forms are supposed to have been alive millions of years ago, and so long a period of time is almost as difficult for the mind to grasp as the idea of eternity or infinity.

p. 43, 1. 3. ***an unhappy metaphor.*** Unhappy because the comparison is misleading. Human laws suggest rules which exercise an artificial control over beings from the outside. The so-called natural laws are the ways in which the various forms of life have evolved.

THE METHOD OF SCIENCE

The method of scientific investigation is nothing but the expression of the necessary mode of working of the human mind. It is simply the mode in which all phenomena are reasoned about, rendered precise and exact. There is just the same kind of difference, between the mental operations of a man of science and those of an ordinary person, as there is between the operations and methods of a baker or of a butcher weighing out his goods in common scales, and the operations of a chemist in performing a difficult and complex analysis by means of his balance and finely graduated weights. It is not that the action of the scales in the one case, and the balance in the other differ in the principles of their construction or manner of working ; but the beam of one is set on an infinitely finer axis than the other, and of course turns by the addition of a much smaller weight.

You will understand this better, perhaps, if I give you some familiar example. You have all heard it repeated, I dare say, that men of science work by means of Induction and Deduction, and that by the help of these operations, they, in a sort of sense, wring from Nature certain other things, which are called Natural Laws, and Causes, and that out of these, by some cunning skill of their own, they build up Hypotheses and Theories. And it is imagined by many, that the operations of the common mind can be by no means compared with these processes, and that they have to be acquired by a sort of special apprenticeship to the craft. To hear all these large words, you would think that the mind of a man of science must be constituted differently from that of his fellow-men; but if you will not be frightened by terms, you will discover that you are quite wrong, and that all these terrible apparatus are being used by yourselves every day and every hour of your lives.

There is a well-known incident in one of Moliere's plays, where the author makes the hero express unbounded delight on being told that he had been talking prose during the whole of his life. In the same way, I trust, that you will take comfort, and be delighted with yourselves, on the discovery that you have been acting on the principles of inductive and deductive philosophy during the same period. Probably there is not one here who has not in the course of the day had occasion to set in motion a complex train of reasoning, of the very same kind, though differing of course in degree, as that which a scientific man goes through in tracing the causes of natural phenomena.

A very trivial circumstance will serve to exemplify this. Suppose you go into a fruiterer's shop, wanting an apple,—you take up one, and, on biting it, you find it is sour ; you look at it, and see that it is hard and green. You take up another one, and that too is hard, green and sour. The shopman offers you a third; but, before biting it, you examine it, and find that it is hard and green, and you immediately say that you will not have it, as it must be sour, like those you have already tried.

Nothing can be more simple than that, you think but if you will take the trouble to analyse and trace out into its logical element what has been done by the mind, you will be greatly surprised. In the first place, you have performed the operation of Induction. You found that, in two experiences, hardness and greenness in apples went together with sourness. It was so in the first case, and it was confirmed by the second. True, it is a very small basis, but still it is enough to make an induction from; you generalize the facts, and you expect to find sourness in apples where you get hardness and greenness. You found upon that a general law, that all hard and green apples are sour ; and that so far as it goes, is a perfect induction. Well, now, suppose, having got your law, that at some time afterwards, you are discussing the qualities of apples with a friend : you will say to him, "It is a very curious thing,—but I find that all hard and green apples are sour !" Your friend says to you "But how do you know that ?" You at once reply, "Oh, because I have tried them over and over again, and have always found them to be so."

Well if we were talking science instead of common sense, we should call that an Experimental Verification. And, if still opposed, you go further, and say, "I have heard from the people in Somersetshire and Devonshire, where a large number of apples are grown, that they have observed the same thing. It is also found to be the case in Normandy, and in North America. In short, I find it to be the universal experience of mankind wherever attention has been directed to the subject." Whereupon, your friend, unless he is a very unreasonable man, agrees with you, and is convinced that you are quite right in the conclusion you have drawn. He believes, although perhaps he does not know he believes it, that the more extensive verifications are,— that the more frequently experiments have been made, and results of the same kind arrived at, that the more varied the conditions under which the same results are attained, the more certain is the ultimate conclusion, and he disputes the question no further. He sees that the experiment has been tried under all sorts of conditions, as to time, place, and people, with the same result ; and he says with you, therefore, that the law you have laid down must be a good one, and he must believe it.

In science we do the same thing ;—the philosopher exercises precisely the same faculties, though in the much more delicate manner. In scientific enquiry it becomes a matter of duty to expose a supposed law to every possible kind of verification and to take care, moreover, that this is done intentionally, and not left to a mere accident, as in the case of the apples. And in science, as in common life, our confidence in a law is in exact proportion to the absence of variation in the result of our experimental verifications.

For instance, if you let go your grasp of an article you may have in your hand, it will immediately fall to the ground. That is a very common verification of one of the best established laws of nature—that of gravitation. The method by which men of science establish the existence of that law is exactly the same as that by which we have established the trivial proposition about the sourness of hard and green apples. But we believe it in such an extensive thorough and unhesitating manner because the universal experience of mankind verifies it, and we can verify it ourselves at any time; and that is the strongest possible foundation on which natural law can rest.

T. H. HUXLEY, *Essays.*

p. 48, 1. 15. ***an infinitely finer axis***—the axis is the middle point of beam, or pivot of the balance. In the balance used by the chemist this is a sharp knife-like edge (generally an agate edge), so that the scale turns to a very tiny weight. Such a balance may be examined in the physics laboratory.

p. 48, 1. 21. ***Induction and Deduction.*** These two processes are explained below.

p. 48, 1. 24. ***Natural Laws.*** Cf. note on preceding passage p. 43, 1. 3.

p. 49, 1. 6. ***craft,*** i.e., of the scientist.

p. 49, 1. 13. ***Moliere,*** a famous French writer of Comedies (1622-1673). The reference is to M. Jourdain in his play *le Bourgeois Gentilhomme.*

p. 50, 1. 6. ***logical elements***—the starting-points of the various processes of reasoning performed by the mind.

p. 50, 1. 13. ***you generalize the facts***—you apply what is true in several instances to all instances of the same class.

p. 51, 1. 23. ***intentionally, and not left to a mere accident***—i.e., that the investigation has been undertaken deliberately, with a definite purpose in view.

p. 51, 1. 26. ***in exact proportion.....verification.*** Our confidence in the truth or soundness of a law depends upon the amount of confirmation we are able to extract from the series of tests we make to verify it.

THE STRUGGLE FOR EXISTENCE

Many cases are on record showing how complex and unexpected are the checks and relations between organic beings which have to struggle together in the same country. I will give only a single instance, which, though a simple one, has interested me. In Staffordshire, on the estate of a relation, where I had ample means of investigation, there was a large and extremely barren heath, which had never been touched by the hand of man; but several hundred acres of exactly the same nature had been enclosed twenty-five years previously and planted with Scotch fir. The change in the native vegetation of the planted part of the heath was most remarkable, more than generally seen in passing from one quite different soil to another : not only the proportional numbers of the heath-plants were wholly changed, but twelve species of plants (not counting grasses and canes) flourished in the plantations, which could not be found on the heath. The effect on the insects must have been still greater, for six insectivorous birds were very common in the plantation, which were not to be seen on the heath; and the heath was frequented by two or three distinct insectivorous birds. Here we see how powerful has been the effect of the introduction of a single tree, nothing whatever else having been done, with the exception that the land had been enclosed, so that cattle could not enter. But how important an element enclosure is, I plainly saw near Farnham, in Surrey. Here there are extensive heaths, with a few clumps of old scotch firs on the distant hill-tops : within the last ten years large spaces have been enclosed, and self-sown firs are now springing up in multitudes, close together that all cannot live. When I ascertained that these young trees had not been sown or planted, I was so much surprised at their numbers that I went to several points of view, whence I could examine hundreds of acres of the unenclosed heath and literally I could not see a single Scotch fir, except the old planted clumps. But on looking closely between the stems of the heath, I found a multitude of seedlings and little trees, which had been perpetually browsed down by the cattle. In one square yard at a point some hundred yards distant from one of the old clumps, I counted thirty-two little trees ; and one of them, with twenty-six rings of growth, had during many years tried to raise its head above the stems of the heath, and had failed. No wonder that as soon as the land was enclosed, it become thickly clothed with vigorously growing young firs. Yet the heath was so extremely barren and so extensive that no one would ever have imagined that cattle would have so closely and effectually searched it for food.

Here we see that cattle absolutely determine the existence of the Scotch fir; but in several parts of the world insects determine the existence of cattle. Perhaps Paraguay offers the most curious instance of this; for here neither cattle nor horses nor dogs have ever run wild, though they swarm southward and northward in a wild state; and it has been proved that this is caused by the greater number of a certain fly in Paraguay, which lays its eggs on the navels of these animals when first born. The increase of these flies, numerous as they are, must be habitually checked by some means, probably by birds. Hence, if certain insectivorous birds (whose numbers are probably regulated by hawks or beasts of prey) were to increase in Paraguay, the flies would decrease—then cattle and horses would become wild, and this would certainly greatly alter (as indeed I have observed in certain parts of South America) the vegetation : this again would largely affect the insects; and this, as we have just seen in Staffordshire, the insectivorous birds, and so on, the relations and changes becoming more and more complicated. We began with insectivorous birds, and we have ended with them. Not that in nature the relations can ever be as simple as this. Battle within battle must ever be recurring with varying success; and yet in the long-run the forces are so nicely balanced, that the face of nature remains uniform for long periods of time, though assuredly the merest trifle would often give the victory to one organic being over another. Nervertheless, so profound is our ignorance. and so high our presumption, that we marvel when we hear of the extinction of an organic being ; and as we do not see the cause, we attribute such a disappearance to some general disaster that has overtaken the world, or invent laws on the duration of the forms of life.

I am tempted to give one more instance showing how plants and animals, most remote in nature, are linked together by a series of complex relations. I shall hereafter have occasion to show that the exotic Lobelia fulgens, in this part of England, is never visited by insects, and consequently, from its peculiar structure, never can set a seed. Many orchids absolutely require the visits of the moths to remove their pollen masses, and thus to fertilize them. From experiments which I have lately tried, I have found that the visits of bees are necessary for the fertilization of some kinds of clover; but humble-bees alone visit the red clover (Trifolium pratense), as other bees cannot reach the nectar. Hence I have very little doubt, that if the whole genus of humble-bees became extinct or very rare in England, the red clover would become very rare, or wholly disappear. The number of humble-bees in any district depends in a great degree on the number of field-mice, which destroy their combs and nests; and Mr. H. Newman, who has long attended to the habits of humble- bees, believes that "more than two-thirds of them are thus destroyed all over England." Now the number of mice is largely dependent, as everyone knows, on the number of cats ; and Mr. Newman says, "Near villages and small towns I have found nests of humble bees more numerous than elsewhere, which I attribute to the number of cats that destroy the mice ?" Hence it is quite credible that the presence of a feline animal in large numbers in a district might determine, through the intervention first of mice and then of bees, the frequency of certain flowers in that district !

CHARLES DARWIN, *On the Origin of Species.*

Charles Darwin (1809-1882) was, along with A R. Wallace (1823-1882), the first to demonstrate how different species of plants and animals come into being. A constant struggle is always going on in nature, and it is often due apparently to chance that certain spaces survive and others die. In this passage Darwin gives an example of this, showing how the enclosure of a piece of ground made that ground favourable for fir trees to survive, and their survival made it possible for other plants to exist within the same enclosure; these in their turn affording food to insects and so to birds. Thus the dependence of different forms of life upon one another is revealed. In Northern India these phenomena may be observed on the "usar" plains : when man cuts down the "babool" trees and the "dhak" jungle, he makes it impossible for any vegetation to exist : but if the trees are allowed to remain, other plants gradually collect around them, and patches of the barren ground gradually regain their fertility.

p. 53, 1. 2. ***checks***—the forces which hinder forms of life from surviving or flourishing.

p. 53, 1. 3. ***organic***=living.

p. 53, 1. 8. ***heath***=corresponds much to an uncultivated "maidan" in India. Heath, a heather, is a wild plant which covers such plains in Britain.

p. 53, 1. 11. ***Scotch fir***—a species of tree allied to the pine trees which grow in the Himalayas.

p. 53, 1. 15. ***proportional numbers of the heath-plants***=that is, the heath-plants were in far larger numbers within the enclosure than without.

p. 53, 1. 17. ***canes***—grasses with hollow jointed stems—like the bamboo in India.

p. 53, 1. 20. ***insectivorous***—insect-eating birds—as, for example, the *Nilkaut*.

p. 54, 1. 5. ***Farnham.*** The great military camp—Aldershot—is close to Farnham.

p. 54, 1. 18. ***seedlings***=plants raised from seeds, young tender plants.

p. 54, 1. 22. ***twenty-six rings of growth***=if the trunk of a tree is cut crosswise a number of rings will be observed in the section of the wood : each of those rings represents a year's growth, so that this stunted tree was actually twenty-six years old.

p. 55, 1. 2. ***Paraguay.*** A country in the centre of the southern portion of South America.

p. 55, 1. 12. ***beasts of prey***—e.g., wild cats destroy birds in large numbers.

p. 55, 1. 23. ***Battle within battle***—struggles between the different opposed species, different factors and conditions sometimes favouring one species sometimes another.

p. 55, 1. 29. ***so high our presumption***= so great is our confidence in our own knowledge.

p. 55, 1. 32. ***we attribute such a disappearance.......of the forms of life.*** Formerly geologists were in the habit of attributing the disappearance of certain forms of animal life to sudden catastrophes, such as the submerging of a continent, or a rapid change in climate, such as the great "Ice Ages." These occurrences are now supposed to have been exceedingly, almost imperceptibly, slow processes. Geologists have also attempted to calculate the length of the periods during which the various forms of plants and animals, know extinct, flourished. These periods are estimated at millions of years, and are now recognised as problematical.

p. 56, 1. 4. ***are linked together by a series of complex relations***=that is to say, two living forms may depend upon one another for their existence, although the causes which bring about this dependence may be very complicated and by no means obvious at first sight.

p. 56, 1. 7. ***Lobelia fulgens.*** Scientists generally give plants and animals two names : the first *(Lobelia)* denotes the family, the second *(fulgens)* denotes the species. Latin is used for these names as it has become a universal language among scientists, so that these scientific Latin names are understood all over the world.

p. 56, 1. 11. ***pollen masses.***—pollen is the fine powder-like substance discharged from the stamens of flowers ; this has to be conveyed to the *ovules* or rudimentary seeds in order that the latter may become fertilized and that the seeds may germinate. This fertilization is often done by the aid of insects.

p. 56, 1. 14. ***clover*** is a fodder plant. The red clover is called *treparta or chitbatta* in N. India.

p. 56, 1. 14. ***humble-bees***—a large species of bee.

p. 56, 1. 31. ***feline animals***—animals belonging to the cat family.

12

Effects of Use and Disuse

FROM the facts alluded to in the first chapter, I think there can be little doubt that use in our domestic animals strengthens and enlarges certain parts, and disuse diminishes them; and that such modifications are inherited. Under free nature, we can have no standard of comparison, by which to judge of the effects of long-continued use or disuse, for we know not the parent-forms; but many animals have structures which can be explained by the effects of disuse. As Professor Owen has remarked, there is no greater anomaly in nature than a bird that cannot fly; yet there are several in this state. The logger-headed duck of South America can only flap along the surface of the water, and has its wings in nearly the same condition as the domestic duck. As the larger ground-feeding birds seldom take flight except to escape danger, I believe that the nearly wingless condition of several birds, which now inhabit or have lately inhabited several oceanic islands, tenanted by no beast of prey, has been caused by disuse. The ostrich indeed inhabits continents and is exposed to danger from which it cannot escape by flight, but by kicking it can defend itself from enemies, as well as any of the smaller quadrupeds. We may imagine that the early progenitor of the ostrich had habits like those of a bustard, and that as natural selection increased in successive generations the size and weight of its body, its legs were used more, and its wings less, until they became incapable of flight.

In some cases we might easily put down to disuse modifications of structure which are wholly, or mainly, due to natural selection. Mr. Wollaston has discovered the remarkable fact that 200 beetles, out of the 550 species inhabiting Madeira, are so far deficient in wings that they cannot fly; and that of the twenty-nine indigenous families no less than twenty-three genera have all to heir species in this condition ! Several facts, namely, that beetles in many parts of the world are frequently blown to sea and perish ; that the beetles in Madeira, as observed by Mr. Wollaston, lie much concealed, until the wind lulls and the sun shines ; that the proportion of wingless beetles is larger on the exposed desert tracts than in Madeira itself; and especially the extraordinary fact, so strongly insisted on by Mr. Wollaston, of the almost entire absence of certain large groups of beetles, elsewhere excessively numerous, which groups have habits of life almost necessitating frequent flight; all these considerations have made me believe that the wingless condition of so many Madeira beetles is mainly due to the action of natural selection, but combined probably with disuse. For during thousands of successive generations each individual beetle which flew least either from its wings having been ever so little less perfectly developed or from indolent habit, will have had the best chance of surviving from not being blown out to sea ; and, on the other hand, those beetles which most readily took to flight would oftenest have been blown to sea and thus have been destroyed.

The insects in Madeira which are not ground-feeders, and which, as the flower-feeding beetles and butterflies, must habitually use their wings to gain their subsistence, have, as Mr. Wollaston suspects their wings not at all reduced, but even enlarged. This is quite in accordance with the action of natural selection. For when a new insect first arrived on the island, the tendency of natural selection to enlarge or to reduce the wings would depend on whether a greater number of individuals were saved by successfully battling with the winds or by giving up the attempt and rarely or never flying. As with mariners shipwrecked near a coast, it would have been better for the good swimmers if they had been able to swim still further, whereas it would have been better for the bad swimmers if they had not been able to swim at all and had stuck to the wreck.

The eyes of moles and of some burrowing rodents are rudimentary in size, and in some cases are quite covered up by skin and fur. This state of the eyes is probably due to gradual reduction from disuse, but aided perhaps by natural selection. In South America, a burrowing rodent, the tuco-tuco, is even more subterranean in its habits than the mole ; and I was assured by a Spaniard, who had often caught them, that they were frequently blind; one which I kept alive was certainly in this condition; the cause, as appeared on dissection, having been inflammation of the inner portion of the eyelids. As frequent inflammation of the eyes must be injurious to any animal, and as eyes are certainly not indispensable to animals with subterranean habits, a reduction in their size with the adhesion of the eyelids and growth of fur over them, might in such case be an advantage ; and if so, natural selection would constantly aid the effects of disuse.

It is well-known that several animals, belonging to the most different classes, which inhabit the caves of Styria and of Kentucky, are blind. In some of the crabs the foot-stalk for the eye remains, though the eye is gone ; the stand for the telescope is there, though the telescope with its glasses has been lost. As it is difficult to imagine that eyes, thought useless, could be in any way injurious to animals living in darkness, I attribute their loss wholly to disuse. In one of the blind animals, namely, the cave-rat, the eyes are of immense size; and Professor Silliman thought that it regained, after living some days in the light, some slight power of vision. In the same manner as in Madeira the wings of some of the insects have been enlarged, and the wings of others have been reduced by natural selection aided by use and disuse, so in the case of the cave-rat natural selection seems to have struggled with the loss of light and to have increased the size of the eyes ; whereas with all the other inhabitants of the caves, disuse by itself seems to have done its work.

CHARLES DARWIN, *On the Origin of Species.*

This and the preceding passage are admirable examples of the straightforward and accurate statement of what has been carefully and patiently observed. Darwin, an almost excessively modest man, admitted in himself an unusual power "in noticing things which easily escape attention, and in observing them carefully."

p. 60, 1. 4. ***such modifications are inherited*** = such changes in the structure of the animals are reproduced in their descendants.

p. 60, 1. 5. ***free nature*** = nature in the wild state as opposed to animals or plants which have been domesticated or cultivated.

p. 60, 1. 12. ***logger-headed duck***—a species of duck with a specially large head.

p. 60, 1. 16. ***ground-feeding birds***=birds which obtain their food entirely from the ground, such as the "peacock."

p. 60, 1. 18. ***birds.....oceanic islands.*** Darwin means birds like the penguins, which are totally unable to fly. Large numbers of these birds were ruthlessly destroyed for their plumage during the nineteenth century. Laws have now been made to protect them. Penguins are found of the islands of the North Atlantic and Pacific Oceans.

p. 61, 1. 1. ***progenitor***=ancestor.

p. 61, 1. 2. ***bustard***=a large, heavy bird, found in certain districts of India, which feeds on the ground but still is capable of strong flight. It is known in parts of India as *Houbara.*

p. 61, 1. 2. ***natural selection***=his process is explained below. The theory has been much disputed by recent scientists.

p. 61, 1. 10. ***Madeira***—an island off the north-west coast of Africa.

p. 61, 1. 13. ***genera***=families. Plants and animals are divided by scientists first into families or genera, that is group which have certain similarities in their structure; thus lions, tigers, leopards belong to the cat family or genus. These families are sub-divided into species, i.e., tiger, lion, leopard.

p. 61, 1. 20. ***desert tracts***—that is, of the continent of Africa.

p. 62, 1. 23. ***moles***—a small burrowing animal with velvety fur and small eyes found in Europe: it is a *rodent*, that is, an animal with strong front (incisor) teeth, and no canine teeth. Canine teeth are developed only in animals that eat flesh.

p. 62, 1. 24. ***rudimentary***=not strongly developed, imperfectly adapted for use.

p. 63, 1. 7. ***adhesion***= "sticking to." What is meant here is that the eyelids become less flexible and tend to cover permanently a larger portion of the eye.

p. 63, 1. 13. ***Styria***—a province in the south-west of Austria.

p. 63, 1. 13. ***Kentucky***—a state in the middle east of the United States of America.

p. 63, 1. 14. ***foot-stalk***=a fleshy attachment in the end of which the eye is situated. Crabs have the power of drawing in or putting out these foot-stalks.

13

The Glow-worm

FEW insects in our climes vie in popular fame with the glow-worm, that curious little animal which to celebrate the little joys of life, kindles a beacon at its tail-end. Who does not know it, at least by name ? Who has not seen it roam amid the grass like a spark fallen from the moon at its full ? The Greeks of old called it by a word meaning the bright tailed. Science employs the same term : it call it the lantern-bearer, *Lampyris noctiluca*. In this case the common name is inferior to the scientific phrase, which, when translated, becomes both expressive and accurate.

In fact, we might easily cavil at the word "worm". The Lampyris is not a worm at all, not even in general appearance. He has six short legs, which he well knows how to use; he is a gad-about, a trot about. In the adult state the male is correctly garbed in wing-cases, like the true Beetle that he is. The female is an ill-favoured thing who know naught of the delights of flying : all her life long she retains the larval shape, which, for the rest, it similar to that of the male, who himself is imperfect so long as he has not achieved the maturity that comes with pairing-time. Even in this initial stage the word "worm" is out of place. We French have the expression "Naked as a worm" to point to the lack of any defensive covering. Now the Lampyris is clothed, that is to say, he wears an epidermis of some consistency; moreover, he is rather richly coloured : his body is dark brown all over, set off with pale pink on the thorax, especially on the lower surface. Finally, each segment is decked at the hinder edge with two spots of a fairly bright red. A costume like this was never worn by a worm.

Let us leave this ill-chosen denomination and ask ourselves what the Lampyris feeds upon. That master in the art of gastronomy, Brillat-Savarin, said : "Show me what you eat and I will tell you what you are."

A similar question should be addressed, by way of a preliminary, to every insect whose habits we propose to study, for, from the least to the greatest in the zoological progression, the stomach sways the world; the data supplied by food are the chief of all the documents of life. Well, in spite of his innocent appearance, the Lampyris is an eater of flesh, a hunter of game; and he follows his calling with rare villainy. His regular prey is the Snail.

This detail has long been known to entomologists. What is not so well-known, what is not known at all yet, to judge by what I have read, is the curious method of attack, of which I have seen no other instance anywhere.

Before he begins to feast, the Glow-worm administers an anesthetic : he chloroforms his victim, rivalling in the process the wonders of our modern surgery, which renders the patient insensible before operating on him. The usual game is a small Snail hardly the size of a cherry, such as, for instance, *Helix variabilis*, who, in the hot weather, collects in clusters on the stiff stubble and other long, dry stalks by the road-side and there remains motionless, in profound meditation, throughout the scorching summer days. It is in some such resting-place as this that I have often been privileged to light upon the Lampyris banqueting on the prey which he had just paralysed on its shaky support by the surgical artifices.

But he is familiar with other preserves. He frequents the edges of the irrigating ditches, with their cool soil, their varied vegetation, a favourite haunt of the Mollusc. Here, he treats the game on the ground ; and, under these conditions, it is easy for me to rear him at home and to follow the operator's performance down to the smallest detail.

I will try to make the reader a witness of the strange sight. I place a little grass in a wide-glass jar. In this I instal a few Glow-worms and a provision of snails of a suitable size, neither too large nor too small, chiefly, *Helix variabilis.* We must be patient and wait. Above all we must keep an assiduous watch, for the desired events come unexpectedly and do not last long.

Here we are at last. The Glow-worm for a moment investigates the prey, which, according to its habit, is wholly withdrawn in the shell, except the edge of the mantle, which projects slightly. Then the hunter's weapon is drawn, a very simple weapon, but one that cannot be plainly perceived without the aid of a lens. It consists of two mandibles bent back powerfully into a hook, very sharp and as thin as a hair. The microscope reveals the presence of a slender groove running throughout the length. And that is all.

The insect repeatedly taps the Snail's mantle with its instrument. It all happens with such gentleness as to suggest kisses rather than bites. As children, teasing one another, we used to talk of "tweaksies" to express a slight squeeze of the finger-tips, something more like a tickling than a serious pinch. Let us use that word. In conversing with animals, language loses nothing by remaining juvenile. It is the right way for the simple to understand one another.

The Lampyris doles out his tweaks. He distributes them methodically, without hurrying, and takes a brief rest after each of them, as though he wished to ascertain the effect produced. Their number is not great : half a dozen, at most, to subdue to prey and deprive it of all power of movement. That other pinches are administered later, at the time of eating, seems very likely, but I cannot say anything for certain, because the sequel escapes me. The first few, however—there are never many—are enough to impart inertia and loss of all feeling to the Mollusc, thanks to the prompt, I might almost say lightning, methods of the Lampyris, who, beyond a doubt, instils some poison or other by means of his grooved hooks.

Here is the proof of the sudden efficacy of those twitches, so mild in appearance : I take the Snail from the Lampyris, who has operated on the edge of the mantle some four or five times. I prick him with a fine needle in the fore-part, which the animal, shrunk into its shell, still leaves exposed. There is no quiver of the wounded tissues, no reaction against the brutality of the needle. A corpse itself could not give fewer signs of life.

Here is something even more conclusive : chance occasionally gives me Snails attacked by the Lampyris while they are creeping along, the foot slowly crawling, the tentacles swollen to their full extent. A few disordered movements betray a brief excitement on the part of the Mollusc and then everything ceases : the foot no longer slugs ; the front part loses its graceful swan-neck curve ; the tentacles become limp and give way under their own weight, dangling feebly like a broken stick. This condition persists.

Is the Snail really dead ? Not at all, for I can resuscitate the seeming corpse at will. After two or three days of that singular condition which is no longer life and yet not death, I isolate the patient and, though this is not really essential to success. I give him a douche which will represent the shower so dear to the able-bodied Mollusc. In about a couple of days, my prisoner, but lately injured by the Glow-worm's treachery, is restored to his normal state. He revives, in a manner; he recovers movement and sensibility. He is affected by the stimulus of a needle; he shifts his place, crawls, puts out his tentacles, as though nothing unusual had occurred. The general torpor, a sort of deep drunkenness, has vanished outright. The dead returns to life. What name shall we give to that form of existence which, for a time, abolishes the power of movement and the sense of pain? I can see but one that is approximately suitable: anæsthesia. The exploits of a host of Wasps whose flesh-eating grubs are provided with meat that is motionless though not dead have taught us the skilful art of the paralyzing insect, which numbs the locomotory nerve- centres with its venom. We have now a humble little animal that first produces complete anæsthesia in its patient. Human science did not in reality invent this art, which is one of the wonders of latter-day surgery. Much earlier, far back in the centuries, the Lampyris, and, apparently, others knew it as well. The animal's knowledge had a long start of ours; the method alone has changed. Our operators proceed by making us inhale the fumes of ether or chloroform; the insect proceeds by injecting a special virus that comes from the mandibular fangs in infinitesimal doses. Might we not one day be able to benefit from this hint? What glorious discoveries the future would have in store for us, if we understood the beastie's secrets better!

J.H. FABRE, *The Wonders of Instinct.*

This passage, translated from the French of the great naturalist. J.H. Fabre, is an admirable example, both of his wonderful patience and accuracy in observing the habits of wild creatures, especially insects, and also of his brilliant power of description. The extract is taken from his work *The Wonders of Instinct,* translated by A.T. de Mattos, by permission of the publishers, Messrs. T. Fisher Unwin, Ltd.

p. 66, 1. 6. ***gad-about*** = one given to wandering about idly.

p. 66, 1. 21. ***larval shape***—the female remains all her life in the wingless grub state. Most insects after emerging from the egg go through three stages of existence: (1) the *larva,* caterpillar or grub stage, (2) the *pupa* or chrysalis stage, (3) the *papiliv* or winged stage.

p. 67, 1. 5. ***epidermis*** = outer layer of skin.

p. 67, 1. 7. ***thorax*** = literally chest, the middle portion of an insect's body which consists of three parts—head, thorax and abdomen.

p. 67, 1. 14. ***gastronomy*** = the science of food.

p. 67, 1. 20. ***progression*** = scale.

p. 67, 1. 20. ***the stomach sways the world***= habits develop out of the necessity imposed upon it in procuring the food it eats.

p. 67, 1. 26. ***entomologists***= those who study entomology—the science dealing with insects.

p. 68, 1. 12. ***surgical artifices,*** i.e., his skill in administering an anæsthetic.

p. 68, 1. 14. ***preserves*** = literally enclosed places where game is preserved for hunting: so "hunting grounds".

p. 68, 1. 17. ***mollusc*** = an animal living in a shell; here= the snail.

p. 68, 1. 17. ***treats*** = "deals with."

p. 68, 1. 32. ***mantle*** = an outer fold of skin in molluscs enclosing the interior organs.

p. 69, 1. 3. ***mandibles*** = jaws — or teeth — called at the end of the passage "mandibular fangs."

p. 69, 1. 28. ***inertia*** = loss of motion.

p. 70, 1. 7. ***reaction against***= shrinking movement from.

p. 70, 1. 13. ***tentacles*** = feelers — long slender appendages which the snail puts out for exploration or when moving.

p. 70, 1. 15. ***douche*** = a pouring of cold water over an animal.

p. 70, 1. 26. ***able-bodied*** = in a normal state of health.

p. 71, 1. 6. ***anæsthesia*** = insensibility.

p. 71, 1. 10. ***locomotory nerve-centres*** — the groups of closely connected nerve cells which convey impulses of sensation and motion to various parts of the body.

p. 71, 1. 20. ***virus*** = poison.

14

Thoreau's Visitor

A MORE simple and natural man it would be hard to find. Vice and disease which are the cause of so much unhappiness in the world, seemed to have hardly any existence for him. He was about twenty-eight years old, and had left Canada and his father's house a dozen years before to work in the United States, and earn money to buy a farm with at last, perhaps in his native country. He was cast in the coarsest mould, a stout but sluggish body, yet gracefully carried, with a thick sunburnt neck, dark bushy hair, and dull, sleepy blue eyes, which were occasionally lit up with expression. He wore a flat grey cloth cap, a dingy great coat, and cowhide boots. He was a great consumer of meat, usually carrying his dinner to his work a couple of miles past my house—for the chopped all summer—in tin a can; cold meats and coffee in a stone bottle which dangled by a string from his belt; and sometimes he offered me a drink. He came along early, crossing my bean-field, though without anxiety or haste to get to his work, such as Yankees exhibit. He wasn't a-going to hurt himself. He didn't care if he only earned his board.

He was a skilful chopper, and indulged in some flourishes and ornaments in his art. He cut his trees level and close to the ground, that the sprouts which came up afterwards might be more vigorous and a sled might slide over the stumps.

He interested me because he was so quiet and solitary, and so happy withal; a well of good-humour and contentment which overflowed at his eyes. His mirth was without alloy. Sometimes I saw him at his work in the woods, felling trees, and he would greet me with a laugh of inexpressible satisfaction, and a salutation in Canadian French, though he spoke English as well. When I approached him he would suspend his work, and with half-suppressed mirth lie along the trunk of a pine which he had felled, and, peeling off the inner bark, roll it up into a ball and chew it while he laughed and talked. Such an exuberance of animal spirits had he that he sometimes tumbled down and rolled on the ground with laughter at anything which made him think and tickled him. Looking round upon the trees he would exclaim— "By George"! I can enjoy myself well-enough here chopping; I want no better sport." Sometimes, when at leisure, he amused himself all day in the woods with a pocket pistol, firing salutes to himself at regular intervals as he walked. In the winter we had a fire by which at noon he warmed his coffee in a kettle; and as he sat on a log to eat his dinner, the chickadees would sometimes come round and alight on his arm and peck at the potato in his fingers; and he said that he "liked to have the little *fellers* about him."

In him the animal man chiefly was developed. In physical endurance and contentment he was causing to the pine and the rock. I asked him once if he was not sometimes tired at night, after working all day; and he answered with a sincere and serious look, "I never was tired in my life." But the intellectual and what is called spiritual man in him were slumbering as in an infant. He had been instructed only in that innocent and ineffectual way in which the Catholic priests teach the aborigines, by which the pupil is never educated to the degree of consciousness, but only the degree of trust and reverence, and a child is not made a man, but kept a child. When Nature made him, she gave him a strong body and contentment for his portion, and propped him on every side with reverence and reliance, that he might live out his three score years and ten a child. He was so genuine and unsophisticated that no introduction would serve to introduce him, more than if you introduced a woodchuck to your neighbour. He would not play any part. Men paid him wages for work, and so helped to feed and clothe him; but he never exchanged opinions with them. He was so simple and naturally humble—if he can be called humble who never aspires—that humility was no distinct quality in him, nor could he conceive of it. Wiser men were demigods to him. He particularly reverenced the writer and the preacher. Their performances were miracles. When I told him that I wrote considerably, he thought for a long time that it was merely the handwriting which I meant, for he could write a remarkably good hand himself. I sometimes found the name of his native parish handsomely written in the snow by the highway, with the proper French accent, and knew that he had passed that way. I asked him if he ever wished to write his thoughts. He said that he had read and written letters for those who could not, but he never tried to write thoughts—no, he could not, he could not tell what to put first, it would kill him, and then there was spelling to be attended to at the same time!

I heard that a distinguished wise man and reformer asked him if he did not want the world to be changed; but he answered with a chuckle of surprise, not knowing that the question had ever been entertained before, "No, I like it well-enough." It would have suggested many things to a philosopher to have dealings with him. To a stranger he appeared to know nothing of things in general; yet I sometimes saw in him a man whom I had not seen before, and I did not know whether he was as wise as Shakespeare or as simply ignorant as a child — whether to suspect him of a fine poetic consciousness or of stupidity. A townsman told me that when he met him sauntering through the village in his small close-fitting cap, and whistling to himself, he reminded him of prince in disguise.

His only books were an almanac and an arithmetic, in which last he was considerably expert. The former was sort of encyclopædia to him, which he supposed to contain an abstract of human knowledge, as indeed it largely does.

One winter day I asked him if he was always satisfied with himself, wishing to suggest to him some higher motive for living, "Satisfied!" said he, "some men are satisfied with one thing and some with another. One man, perhaps, if he has go enough, will be satisfied to sit all day with his bar to the fire and his belly to the table, by George Yet I never, by any maneuvring, could get him take the spiritual view of things; the highest that he appeared to conceive of was a simple expedience such as you might expect an animal to appreciate and this, practically, is true of most men. If suggested any improvement in his mode of life, he merely answered, without expressing any regret, that it was too late. Yet he thoroughly believed honesty and the like virtues.

H.D. THOREAU, *Walden*.

At Harvard University Thoreau (1817-1862) confined his studies almost entirely to natural history and to classical and oriental literature. In 1845 he retired from society to live his own resources in simplicity and comparative solitude. One passage, which is from his best-know book *Walden*, describes one of the acquaintances he made during his two years' sojourny in his little hut by the pond in the woods. "Thoreau's power of observation," says his friend Emerson, "seemed to indicate additional senses. He saw as with microscope, heard as with ear trumpet, and his memory was a photographic register of what he saw and heard."

p. 74, 1. 8. ***He was cast in the coarsest mould-*** his general physical appearance was entirely lacking in refinement.

p. 74, 1. 12. ***lit up with expression—*** his eyes usually do occasionally became bright, showing intelligence, when his interest was aroused.

p. 74, 1. 16. ***chopped*** = cut down trees.

p. 74, 1. 21. ***Yankees.*** The Americans of the United States have always been remarkable for their business-like instincts, and for their dislike of wasting time.

p. 74, 1. 24. ***indulged in some .... ornaments*** — he was in the habit of displaying his skill and dexterity with some ostentation.

p. 75, 1. 4. ***sled*** = sledge — the stumps were cut level with the ground with such skill that a sledge could pass easily over them.

p. 75, 1. 6. ***well of good-humour ... eyes.*** He was perfectly contented and good-humoured, and these feelings could not help expressing themselves in his eyes, i.e., they were expressed in the look in his eyes.

p. 75, 1. 8. ***without alloy*** = lit, without being mixed with an inferior metal. So here his mirth was pure and unmixed with any other feelings, e.g., contempt or anger.

p. 75, 1. 11. ***Canadian French.*** The French were the first to colonise Canada. The capital Quebec was captured by the British under General Wolfe in 1759, and Canada was ceded to Great Britain in 1763. But the French-Canadians retained their customs, laws, religion and language: a dialect of French is still spoken in the Quebec province.

p. 75, 1. 20. ***tickled him*** = amused him.

p. 75, 1. 24. ***firing salutes to himself,*** *not* saluting himself but firing salutes for his own amusement — on the analogy of "talking to himself."

p. 75, 1. 28. ***chickadees.*** A small American bird (the Black-capped Titmouse).

p. 75, 1. 31. ***fellers.*** Colloquial for "fellows."

p. 76, 1. 1. ***cousin to the pine and the rock*** = he had the qualities, i.e., endurance, contentment with his lot in life, usually attributed to natural objects like pine trees or rocks.

p. 76, 11. 5-7. ***But the intellectual...slumbering as in an infant*** = but his intellect was no more developed, and his apprehension of religion was no greater than an infant's.

p. 76, 1. 15. ***propped him with reverence and reliance.*** Nature bestowed on him these two qualities which made him as innocent and happy as a child.

p. 76, 1. 16. ***three score years and ten*** — the average length of man's life according to the Psalmist in the Old Testament. Cf. Psalm xc, 10.

p. 76, 1. 19. ***woodchuck*** = a kind of squirrel.

p. 76, 1. 20. ***He would not play any part*** = he would not behave in any way that was not natural to him. He would act and say exactly what he felt.

p. 76, 1. 26. demigods = seemed to him to the partially divine, as their wisdom was so far beyond his reach.

p. 77, 1. 2. ***proper French accent.*** There are three accents in French — his putting the correct accent on the word shows that he had acquired a thorough proficiency in writing.

p. 77, 1. 7. ***it would kill him.*** A common expression implying that the exertion caused would be greater than he could bear.

p. 77, 1. 17. ***a man whom I had not seen before.*** He sometimes revealed a nature such as I had never come across before.

p. 77, 1. 28. ***an abstract*** — a summary. Thoreau is thinking of almanacs like *Whitaker's Almanac* or the *Indian Year Book* which contain information on a variety of subjects.

p. 78, 1. 7. ***a simple expediency*** — he considered that a man's first object in life was simply to seek what was advantageous to himself.

GEORGE BORROW AND THE FLAMING TINMAN

"You need not be afraid," said I, addressing myself to the man, "I mean you no harm; I am a wanderer like yourself — come here to seek for shelter — you need not be afraid. Good day to you, brother ; I bid you welcome."

The man eyed me suspiciously for a moment, then, turning to his horse with a loud curse, he pulled him up from his haunches, and led him and the cart farther down to one side of the dingle, muttering as he passed me, "Afraid. H'm !"

I do not remember ever to have seen a more ruffianly-looking fellow; he was about six feet high, with an immensely athletic frame; his face was black and buff, and sported an immense pair of whiskers, but with here and there a grey hair, for his age could not be much under fifty. He wore a faded blue frock-coat and corduroys — on his black head was a kind of red night-cap, round his bull neck a Barcelona handkerchief—I did not like the look of the man at all.

"Afraid," growled the fellow, proceeding to unharness his horse; "that was the word, I think."

But other figures were now already upon the scene. Dashing past the other horse and cart, which by this time had reached the bottom of the pass, appeared an exceedingly tall woman, or rather girl for she could scarcely have been above eighteen; she was dressed in a tight bodice, and a blue gown hat, bonnet, or cap she had none, and her hair, which was flaxen, hung down on her shoulders unconfined; her complexion was fair, and her features handsome, with a determined but frank expression. She was followed by another female, about forty, stout and vulgar-looking, at whom I scarcely glanced, my whole attention being absorbed by the tall girl.

"What's the matter, Jack?" said the latter, looking at the man.

"Only afraid, that's all," said the man, still proceeding with his work.

"Afraid of what—of that lad? Why, he looks like a ghost—I would engage to thrash him with one hand."

"You might beat me with no hands at all," said I, "fair damsel, only by looking at me. I never saw such a face and figure, both regal—why, you look like Ingeborg, Queen of Norway; she had twelve brothers, you know, and could lick them all, though they were heroes."

"None of your chaffing, young fellow," said the tall girl, "or I will give you what shall make you wipe your face; be civil, or you will rue it. Though I keep company with gipsies, I would have you to know that I come of Christian blood and parents, and was born in the great house of Long Melford."

"I have no doubt," said I, "that it was a great house; judging from your size, I shouldn't wonder if you were born in a church."

"Stay, Belle," said the man, putting himself before the young virago, who was about to rush on me, "my turn is first"; — then advancing to me in a menacing attitude, he said, with a look of deep malignity, " 'Afraid' was the word, wasn't it?"

"It was," said I, "but I think I wronged you; I should have said, aghast, you exhibited every symptom of one laboring under uncontrollable fear."

The fellow stared at me with a look of stupid ferocity, and appeared to be hesitating whether to strike or not; ere he could make up his mind, the tall girl stepped forward, crying, "He's chaffing; let me at him"; and, before I could put myself on my guard, she struck me a blow on the face which nearly brought me to the ground. "Enough," said I, putting my hand to my cheek; "you have now performed your promise and made me wipe my face. Now be pacified, and tell me fairly the grounds of this quarrel."

"Grounds!" said the fellow; "didn't you say I was afraid; and if you hadn't who gave you leave to camp on my ground?"

"Is it your ground?" said I.

"A pretty question," said the fellow, "as if all the world didn't know that. Do you know who I am?"

"I guess I do," said I; "unless I am much mistaken, you are he whom folks call the 'Flaming Tinman.' To tell you the truth, I'm glad we've met, for I wished to see you. These are your two wives, I suppose; I greet them. There's no harm done— there's room enough here for all of us — we shall soon be good friends, I dare say; and when we are a little better acquainted, I'll tell you my history."

"Well, if that doesn't beat all," said the fellow.

"I don't think he's chaffing now," said the girl, whose anger seemed to have subsided on a sudden; "the young man speaks civil enough."

"Civil," said the fellow, with an oath; "but that's just like you; with you it is a blow, and all over. Civil! I suppose you would have him stay here, and get into all my secrets, and hear all I may have to say to my two morts."

"Two morts, " said the girl, kindling up, "where are they?" Speak for one and no more. I am no mort of yours, whatever someone else may be. I tell you one thing, Black John, or Anselo, for t'other ain't your name, the same thing I told the young man here, be civil, or you will rue it."

The fellow looked at the girl furiously, but his glance soon quailed before hers; he withdrew his eyes, and cast them on my little horse, which was feeding among the trees. "What's this," said he, rushing forward and seizing the animal. "Why, as I'm alive, this is the horse of that mumping villain Slingsby."

"It's his no longer; I bought it and paid for it."

"It's mine now," said the fellow; "I swore I would seize it the next time I found it on my beat; ay, and beat the master too."

"I am not Slingsby."

"All's one for that."

"You don't say you will beat me ?"

"Afraid was the word."

"I'm sick and feeble."

"Hold up your fists."

"Wouldn't the horse satisfy you ?"

"Horse nor bellows either."

"No mercy, then."

"Here's at you."

"Mind your eyes, Jack. There, you've got it. I thought so," shouted the girl, as the fellow staggered back from a sharp blow on the eye. "I thought he was chaffing at all along."

"Never more Anselo. You know what to do, go in," said the vulgar woman, who had hitherto not spoken a word, but who now came forward with all the look of a fury; "go in apopli; you'll smash ten like he."

The Flaming Tinman took her advice, and came in bent on smashing, but stopped short on receiving a left-handed blow on the nose.

"You'll never beat the Flaming Tinman in that way," said the girl, looking at me doubtfully.

And so I began to think myself, when, in the twinkling of an eye, the Flaming Tinman disengaged himself of his frock-coat, and, dashing off his red night-cap, came rushing in more desperately than ever. To a flush hit which he received in the mouth he paid as little attention as a wild but would have done; in a moment his arms were around me, and in another, he had hurled me down, falling heavily upon me. The fellow's strength appeared to be tremendous.

"Pay him off now," said the vulgar woman. The laming Tinman made no reply, but planting his knees on my breast, seized my throat with two huge horny hands. I gave myself up for dead, and probably should have been so in another minute but for the tall girl, who caught hold of the handkerchief, which the fellow wore round his neck, with a grasp nearly as powerful as that with which he pressed my throat.

"Do you call that fair play?" said she.

"Hands off, Belle, " said the other woman; "do you call it fair play to interferred? hand off, or I'll be down upon you myself."

But Belle paid no heed to indli injunction, and tugged so hard at the handkerchief that the Flaming Tinman was nearly throttled; suddenly relinquishing his hold on me, he started on his feet, and aimed a blow at my fair preserver, who avoided it, but said coolly:-

"Finish t'other business first, and then I'm your woman whenever you like; but finish it fairly — no foul play when I'm by — I'll be the boy's second, and Moll can pick you up when he happens to knock you down."

The battle during the next ten minutes raged with considerable fury, but it so happened that during this time I was never able to knock the Flaming Tinman down, but on the contrary received six knock-down blows myself. "I can never stand this," I said, as I sat on the knee of Belle, "I am afraid I must give in; the Flaming Tinman hits very hard," and I spat out a mouthful of blood.

"Sure enough you'll never beat the Flaming Tinman in the way you fight — it's of no use flipping at the Flaming Tinman with your left hand; why don't you use your right ?"

"Because I'm not handy with it," said I; and then getting up, In once more confronted the Flaming Tinman, and struck him six blows for his one, but they were all left-handed blows, and the blow which the Flaming Tinman gave me knocked me off my legs.

"Now, will you use Long Melford?" said Belle, picking me up.

"I don't know what you mean by Long Melford," said I, gasping for breath.

"Why, this long right of yours," said Belle, feeling my right arm — "if you do I shouldn't wonder if you yet stood a chance."

And now the Flaming Tinman was once more ready, much more ready than myself. I, however, rose from my second's knee as well as my weakness would permit me; on he came, striking left and right, appearing almost as fresh as to wind and spirit as when he first commenced the combat, though his eyes were considerably swelled, and his nether lip was cut in two; on he came, striking left and right, and I did not like his blows at all, or even the wind of them, which was anything but agreeable, and I gave way before him. At last he aimed a blow, which had it taken full effect, would doubtless have ended the battle, but owing to his slipping, the fist only grazed my left shoulder, and came with terrific force against a tree, close to which I had been driven: before the Tinman could recover himself, I collected all my strength, and struck him beneath the ear, and then fell to the ground completely exhausted, and it so happened that the blow which I struck the tinker beneath the ear was a right-handed blow.

"Hurrah for Long Melford!" I heard Belle exclaim; "there is nothing like Long Melford for shortness all the world over."

At these words, I turned round my head as I lay, and perceived the Flaming Tinman stretched on the ground apparently senseless.

GEORGE BORROW, *Lavengo.*

p. 81, 1. 9. ***dingle*** — a low-lying piece of ground shaded by trees.

p. 81, 1. 14. ***black and buff*** — black because his hair was that colour, and also probably because he was unshaven; buff - a dull yellow was the colour of his skin.

p. 81, 1. 14. ***sported***= displayed.

p. 81, 1. 17. ***corduroys*** = trousers or breeches made of coarse thick-ribbed cotton stuff, usually worn by labourers.

p. 81, 1. 19. ***Barcelona handkerchief.*** A large, richly-coloured handkerchief made at Barcelona in Spain, and worn by Spaniards round the neck.

p. 82, 1. 17 ***he looks like a ghost*** — pale, white. Borrow has just recovered from an illness.

p. 82, 1. 23. ***Ingeborg, Queen of Norway.*** Daughter of Haakon of Norway who married Eric of Sweden. Their son Magnus succeeded to the combined Norwegian and Swedish thrones in 1319.

p. 82, 1. 24. ***lick them.*** — beat them.

p. 82, 1. 26. ***none of your chaffing.*** Stop your bantering (ridiculing).

p. 82, 1. 27. ***I will give... wipe your face.*** I will give your such a blow as will make you rub your face—as she actually did.

p. 82, 1. 29. ***gipsies.*** The word is a corruption of Egyptian, because Egypt was at one time supposed to have been the original home of these wandering tribes. The gipsies gain their living by horse dealing, fortune telling, basket weaving, and mending tin vessels (like the Tinman here). They are found in nearly all European countries, and appear to have come originally from India, as their language, Romany, is nearly akin to Hindi— but their origin is still only obscurely known.

p. 82, 1. 31. ***Long Melford.*** A small town in Suffolk in the east of England. The great house was the workhouse or poorhouse. Later on in the passage Long Melford is used facetiously for a long swinging blow delivered with the right hand.

p. 83, 1. 4. ***virago*** — a woman with the strength and spirit of a man.

p. 83, 1. 26. ***A pretty question*** — that is a fine question — said ironically.

p. 83, 1. 30. ***Flaming Tinman.*** Flaming — probably because of the red night-cap and brightly-coloured handkerchief he wore.

p. 84, 1. 6. ***Well if that doesn't beat all.*** Some such imprecation as "May I be cursed" is to be understood before "if" The meaning is "that is the most astounding or impudent remark of all you have made."

p. 84, 1. 14. ***morts*** — wives in the gipsy language.

p. 84, 1. 18. ***t'other ain't your name.*** The other (Black Jack) isn't your real name.

p. 84, 1. 26. ***mumping*** = sullen.

p. 84, 1. 30. ***beat.*** The special tract of country which the Flaming Tinman considered his own, in which he used to carry on his profession.

p. 85, 1. 1. ***All's one for that.*** It is all the same thing as far as that is concerned. That makes no difference.

p. 85, 1. 17. ***apopli*** = "again" in gipsy language.

p. 85, 1. 28. ***flush hit***= a hit full in the face.

p. 86, 1. 20. ***I'm your woman*** — I am ready to fight you.

p. 87, 1. 2. ***flipping*** — hitting feebly.

p. 87, 1. 27. ***wind of them*** -- the wind they made when they missed me.

p. 88, 1. 8. ***there is nothing ..... shortness.*** A pun on long and short. A long right-handed blow is the best for making short work of your opponent, i.e., beating him in a short time.

COBBETT BECOMES ENGAGED

When I first saw my life, she was *thirteen years old,* and I was within about a month of *twenty-one.* She was the daughter of a Sergeant of artillery, and I was the Sergeant-major of a regiment of foot, both stationed in forts near the city of St. John, in the Province of New-Brunswick. I sat in the same room with her, for about an hour, in company with others, and I made up my mind that she was the very girl for me. That I thought her beautiful is certain, for that I had always said should be an indispensable qualification; but I saw in her what I deemed marks of that sobriety of *conduct* of which I have said so much, and which has been by far the greatest blessing of my life. It was now dead of winter, and, of course, the snow several feet deep on the ground, and the weather piercing cold. It was my habit, when I had done my morning's writing, to go out at break of day to take a walk on a hill at the foot of which our barracks lay. In about three mornings after I had first seem her, I had, by an invitation to breakfast with me, got up two young men to join me in my walk; and the road lay by the house of her father and mother. It was hardly light, but she was out on the snow, scrubbing out a washing-tub. "That's the girl for me," said I when we had got out of her hearing. One of these young men came to England soon afterwards; and he, who keeps an inn in Yorkshire, came over to Preston, at the time of the election, to verify whether I were the same man. When he found that I was he appeared surprised; but what was his surprise, when I told him that all those tall young men, whom he saw around me, were the *sons* of that pretty little girl that he and I saw scrubbing out the washing-tub on the snow in New-Brunswick at day-break in the morning!

From the day that I first spoke to her, I never had a thought of her ever being the wife of any other man, more than I had thought of her being transformed into a chest of drawers; and I formed my resolution at once, to marry her as soon as we could get permission, and to get out of the army as soon as I could. So that this matter was, at once, settled as firmly as if written in the book of fate. At the end, of about six months, my regiment, and I along with it, were removed to Frederickton, a distance of a *hundred miles*, up the river of St. John; and, which was worse, the artillery were expected to go off to England a year or two before our regiment! The artillery went, and she along with them; and now it was that I acted a part of becoming a real and sensible lover. I was aware, that, when she go to that gay place Woolwich, the house of her father and mother, necessarily visited by numerous person not the most select, might become unpleasant her, and I did not like, besides, that she should continue to *work hard.* I had saved a *hundred and fifty guineas,* the earnings of my early hours, in writing for the paymaster, the quartermaster, and others, in addition to the savings of my own pay. *I sent her all my money,* before she sailed; and wrote to her to beg of her, if she found her home uncomfortable, to hire a lodging with respectable people: and, at any rate, not to spare the money, by any means, but to buy herself good clothes, and to live without hard work, until I arrived in England; and I, in order to induce her to lay out the money, told her that I should get plenty more before I came home.

As the malignity of the devil would have it, we were kept abroad *two years longer* than our time, Mr. Pitt (England not being so tame then as she is now) having knocked up a dust with

Spain about Nootka Sound. Oh, how I cursed Nootka Sound, and poor bawling Pitt too, I am afraid ! At the end of *four years,* however, home I came; landed at Portsmouth, and got my discharge from the army by the great kindness of poor Lord Edward Fitzgerald, who was then Major of my regiment. I found my little girl a *servant of all work* (and hard work it was), at *five pounds a year,* in the house of a Captain Brisac; and without hardly saying a word about the matter, she put into my hands *the whole of my hundred and fifty guineas unbroken!*

Need I tell the reader what my feelings were? Need I tell kind-hearted English parents what effect his ancedote *must* have produced on the minds of our children? Need I attempt to describe what effect this example ought to have on every young woman who shall do me the honour to read this book? Admiration of her conduct, and self-congratulation on this indubitable proof of the soundness of my own judgment, were now added to my love of her beautiful person.

Now, I do not say that there are not many young women of this country who would, under similar circumstances, have acted as my wife did in this case; on the contrary, I hope, and do sincerely believe, that there are. But when *her age* is considered; when we reflect, that she was living in a place crowded, literally *crowded,* with gaily-dressed and handsome young men, many of whom really far richer and in higher rank than I was, and scores of them ready to offer her their hand; when we reflect that she was living amongst young women who put upon their backs every shilling that they could come at; when we see her keeping the bag of gold untouched, and working hard to provide herself with but mere necessary apparel, and doing this while she was passing from *fourteen to eighteen years of age;* when we view the whole of the circumstances we must say that here is an example, which, while it reflects honour on her sex, ought to have weigh with every young woman whose eyes or ears this relation shall reach.

W. COBBETT, *Advice to Young Men.*

William Cobbett (1763-1835), who was first a ploughman and then a soldier, became a most prolific and influential writer mainly on political subjects at a momentous period of English history. He was a most inconsistent politician, but his gift of vivid, racy, masculine English gives permanent value to much that he wrote. His *Advice to Young Men* (1830), from which our two autobiographical passages are taken, was addressed primarily to his own sons.

p. 91, 1. 5. ***St. John,*** in the Province of New-Brunswick, Canada.

p. 91, 1. 12. ***of which I have said so much.*** Throughout this book Cobbett has insisted upon sobriety as a wifely ideal: a good wife should be self-controlled, moderate and sedate in her conduct, not wayward or fanciful.

p. 91, 1. 14. ***dead of winter.*** The middle of winter—cf. dead of night: the time when everything is perfectly still. The ordinary operations of life are largely suspended on account of the intense cold, and the snow lying on the ground hinders traffic.

p. 92, 1. 6. ***Preston,*** a town in Lancashire, on the river Ribble.

p. 92, 1. 6. ***the election.*** This was the famous election of 1826, fought on the Reform Bill, which, when it became law, enfranchised the mass of the middle and lower middle class. Cobbett in press and in Parliament was a leading advocate of this reform. Sir Walter Scott (p. 126, 1. 8,) opposed it.

p. 92, 1. 7. ***same man,*** i.e., whom he had known in New-Brunswick.

p. 92, 1. 16. ***being transformed into a chest of drawers.*** An absurd comparison to show the impoosibility of Cobbetts's entertaining any such thought.

p. 92, 1. 30. ***Woolwich,*** on the Thames, now a suburb of London to the east. At the time of which Cobbett writes it was the principal depot for artillery. The Arsenal is still at Woolwich.

p. 92, 1. 32. ***not the most select*** — not the people Cobbett himself would have wished to associate with her.

p. 93, 1. 4. ***paymaster*** — the official who pays the troops.

p. 93, 1. 4. ***quartermaster*** — the officer in the regiment whose duties are the assigning of quarters, the laying out of the camp, looking after rations, ammunition, etc.

p. 93, 1. 12. ***lay out the money*** — spend it.

p. 93, 1. 15. ***As the malignity of the devil would have it.*** A strong phrase for "as ill luck would have it," or "owing to the perversity of fate we were kept...."

p. 93, 1. 17. ***Mr. Pitt having knocked up.....Nootka Sound.*** Mr. Pitt had caused feelings to become strained between England and Spain, and a good deal of excitement had arisen in consequence. The cause was this: In 1789 an English vessel was seized in Nootka Sound in Vancouver Island by two Spanish ships of war, and her crew imprisoned on the ground that a trespass had been committed against the sovereign rights of Spain. In 1790 war seemed certain, but it was avoided through the firm though conciliatory action of Pitt.

p. 93, 1. 20. ***bawling.*** Cobbett, who was a Radical, naturally disliked Pitt. "Bawling" is used contemptuously here, suggesting that Pitt spoke in a noisy fashion to silence opposition—or used forcible or exaggerated language for the same purpose. This was, as a matter of fact, much truer of Cobbett himself than of Pitt.

p. 93, 1. 20. ***poor Lord Edward Fitzgerald.*** Poor because he was dismissed from the army on account of his active sympathy with the French Revolution, and because of his premature death in 1798, due to dangers and hardships incurred as an Irish revolutionary leader.

p. 93, 1. 25. ***servant of all work*** = a servant who did all the work of the house.

p. 93, 1. 31. ***Need I tell... our children.*** This book was written in the first place for his own children. Their mother's example must have made a great impression upon them.

p. 94, 1. 19. ***put upon their backs*** = spent all their money of fine clothes.

COBBETT'S TEMPTATION

Partly from misinformation, and partly from miscalculation, I had lost my way; and, quite alone, but armed with my sword and a brace of pistols, to defend myself against the bears, I arrived at the loghouse in the middle of a moonlight night, the hoar frost covering the trees and the grass. A stout and clamorous dog, kept off by the gleaming of my sword, waked the master of the house, who got up, received me with great hospitality, got me something to eat, and put me into a featherbed, a thing that I had been a stranger to for some years. I, being very tired, had tried to pass the night in the woods, between the trunks of two large trees, which had fallen side by side, and within a yard of each other. I had made a nest for myself of dry fern, and had made a covering by laying boughs of spruce across the trunks of the trees. But unable to sleep on account of the cold; becoming sick from the great quantity of water that I had drunk during the heat of the day, and being, moreover, alarmed at the noise of the bears, and lest one of them should find me in a defenceless state, I had roused myself up, and had crept along as well as I could. So that no hero of Eastern romance ever experienced a more enchanting change.

I had got into the house of one of those Yankee loyalists, who, at the close of the revolutionary war (which, until it had succeeded, was called a rebellion) had accepted of grants of land in the King's Province of New-Brunswick; and who, to the great honour of England, had been furnished with all the means of making new and comfortable settlements. I was suffered to sleep till breakfast time, when I found a table, the like of which I have since seem so many in the United States, loaded with good things. The master and the mistress of the house, aged about fifty, were like what an English farmer and his wife were half a century ago. There were two sons, tall and stout, who appeared to have come in from work, and the youngest of whom was about my age, then twenty-three. But there was another member of the family, aged nineteen, who (dressed according to the neat and simple fashion of New England, whence she had come with her parents five or six years before) had her long light-brown hair twisted neatly up, and fastened on the top of her head, in which head were a pair of lively blue eyes, associated with features of which that softness and that sweetness, so characteristic of American girls, were the predominant expressions, the whole being set off by a complexion indicative of glowing health, and forming, figure, movements, and all taken together, an assemblage of beauties, far surpassing any that I have ever seen but once in my life. That once was, too, two years ago; and, in such a case and at such an age, two years, two whole years, is long, long while!

Here was the present against the absent: here was the power of the eyes pitted against that of the memory: here were all the senses up in arms to subdue the influence of the thoughts: here was vanity, here was passion, here was the spot of all sports in the world, and here was also the life, and the manners and the habits and the pursuits that I delighted in: here was everything that imagination can conceive against the poor little brunette in England! What, then, did I fall in love at once with this bouquet of lilies and roses? Oh! by no means. I was, however, so enchanted with the place: I so much enjoyed its tranquility, the shade of the maple trees, the business of the farm, the sports of the water and of the woods, that I stayed at it to the last possible minute, promising at my departure, to come again as often as I possibly could; a promise which I most punctually fulfilled.

During more than two years I spent all the time I could with my Yankee friends: they were all fond of me: I talked to them about country affairs, my evident delight in which they took as a compliment to themselves: the father and mother treated me as one of their children; the sons as a brother; and the daughter, who was as modest and as full of sensibility as she was beautiful, in a way to which a chap much less sanguine than I was would have given the tenderest interpretation; which treatment I, especially in the last-mentioned case, most cordially repaid.

It is when you meet in company with others of your own age that you are, in love matters, put most frequently to the test, and exposed to detection.The next door neighbour might, in that country, be ten miles off. We used to have a frolic, sometimes at one house and sometimes at another. Here where female eyes are very much on the alert, no secret can long be kept; and very soon father, mother, brothers and the whole neighbourhood looked upon the thing as certain, not excepting herself, to whom I, however, had never once even talked of marriage, and never had even told her that I loved her. But I had a thousand times done these by implication, taking into view the interpretation that she would naturally put upon my looks and acts; and it was of this, that I had to accuse myself.

Yet I was not a deceiver; for my affection for her was very great: I spent no really pleasant hours but with her: I was uneasy if she showed the slightest regard for any other young man: I was unhappy if the smallest matter affected her health or spirits: I quitted her in dejection, and returned to her with eager delight: many a time, when I could get leave but for a day, I paddled in a canoe two whole succeeding nights, in order to pass that day with her. If this was not love, it was first cousin to it, for as to any criminal intention. I no more thought of it, in her case, than if she had been my sister. Many times I put myself the questions: "What am I at? Is not this wrong? Why do I go?" But still I went.

The last parting came; and now came my just punishment! The time was known to everybody, and was irrevocably fixed; for I had to move with a regiment, and the embarkation of a regiment is an epoch in a thinly settled province. To describe this parting would be too painful even at this distant day, and with this frost of age upon my head. The kind and virtuous father came forty miles to see me just as I was going on board in the river. His looks and words I have never forgotten. As the vessel descended, she passed the mouth of that creek which I had so often entered with delight; and though England, and all that England contained, were before me, I lost sight of this creek with an aching heart.

On what trifles turn the great events in the life of man! If I had received a cool letter from my intended wife: if I had only heard a rumour of anything from which fickleness in her might have been inferred; if I had found in her any, even the smallest, abatement of affection; if she had but let go any one of the hundred strings by which she held my heart: if any of these, never would the world have heard of me. Young as I was; able as I was as a soldier; proud as I was of the admiration and commendations of which I was the object; fond as I was, too, of the command, which, at so early an age, my rare conduct and great natural talents had given me; sanguine as was my mind, and brilliant as were my prospects: yet I had seen so much of the meannesses, the unjust partialities, the insolent pomposity, the disgusting dissipations of that way of life, that I was weary of it: I longed, exchanging my fine laced coat for the Yankee farmer's home-spun, to be where I should never behold the supple crouch of servility, and never hear the hectoring voice of authority again; and, on the lonely banks of this branch-covered creek, which contained (she out of the question) everything congenial to my taste and dear to my heart, I, unapplauded, unfeared, unenvied and uncalumniated, should have lived and died.

WILLIAM COBBETT, *Advice to Young Men.*

p. 97, 1. 5. *loghouse* = a house built of logs. Such as are used by the settlers in Canada, who develop the country and clear away the forests, turning forest land into corn land.

p. 97, 1. 10. *feather-bed* = a bed covered with a mattress stuffed with feathers, which is very soft and warm.

p. 97, 1. 16. *spruce* = a species of fir tree—akin to the pine trees of the Himalayas.

p. 98, 1. 2. *revolutionary war.* The American War of Independence (1776-83). In England it was considered a rebellion on the part of the American Colonists.

p. 98, 1. 18. *New England.* A province on the east coast of North America colonized by the English Puritans in the seventeenth century. Its capital was Boston. It now comprises the States of Maine, Vermont, New Hampshire, Massachusetts, Connecticut and Rhode Island.

p. 98, 1. 29. *but once in my life.* For this occasion see the previous passage.

p. 99, 1. 1. *the present against the absent* = the beauty of this girl who was present, and the beauty of the absent girl in England to whom he was engaged, produced a conflict in his mind.

p. 99, 1. 5. *vanity* = his vanity was flattered by the impression he made upon this girl's feelings.

p. 99, 1. 9. *brunette* = a dark-skinned, dark-haired woman.

p. 99, 1. 11. *bouquet of lilies and roses.* This girl had all the beauty that is produced by a fair skin (lilies) and pink cheeks (roses).

p. 99, 1. 14. *maple trees* — the maple belongs to the same family of trees as the *chinar*: maples are common in Canada, and sugar is extracted from them.

p. 99, 1. 27. *chap.* Colloquial = "person" — not used in serious prose.

p. 99, 1. 28. *given the tenderest interpretation* = would have realized that she was in love with him.

p. 100, 1. 3. *frolic* = a merry party — merry making.

p. 101, 1. 2. *is an epoch... province* = is an important date closing a period, *i.e.*, while the regiment is there, life is full of variety; after the regiment has gone life becomes dull and monotonous once more.

p. 101, 1. 20. *the hundred strings* = if any one of the hundred ties or bonds by which I was attached to her had been broken.

p. 101, 1. 21. *if any of these.* An elliptical sentence. "Things had happened" must be understood as following "these".

p. 101, 1, 25. *command* = his position of command as sergeant-major.

p. 101, 1. 30 ***pomposity*** = self- importance.

p. 102, 1. 1. ***home-spun*** = cloth woven at home.

p. 102, 1. 2. ***supple crouch of servility*** = the readiness to bow or bend in a humiliating fashion before one's superiors: as of private soldiers before their officers, or of a person of lower rank generally before a higher.

p. 102, 1. 2. ***hectoring*** = bullying. The word is derived from Hector, the leader of the Trojans in the great Trogan War, who had a blustering manner.

p. 102, 1. 7. ***uncalumniated*** = he would never have had to submit to the abuse which was levelled at him by political writers and others during his later career. He became a noted political writer after his return to England; his principal political work was the journal, *Gobbett's Weekly Political Register,* which he edited from 1802-1835.

THE DESERT

The manner of my daily march was this. At about an hour before dawn, I rose, and made the most of about a print of water which I allowed myself for washing. The I breakfasted upon tea and bread. As soon as the beasts were loaded, I mounted my camel and pressed forward. My poor Arabs being on foot would sometimes moan with fatigue, and pray for rest, but I was anxious to enable them to perform their contract for bringing me to Cairo within the stipulated time, and I did not therefore allow a halt until the evening came. About midday or soon after, Mysseri used to bring up his camel alongside of mine and supply me with a piece of the dried bread softened in water, and also (as long as it lasted) with a piece of the tongue. After this there came into my hand (how well I remember it!) the little tin cup half filled with wine and water.

As long as you are journeying in the interior of the Desert you have no particular point to make for as your resting place. The endless sands yield nothing but small stunted shrubs; even these fail after the first two or three days, and from that time you pass over broad plains—you pass over newly reared hills-you pass through valleys dug out by the last week's storm, and the hills and the valleys are sand, sand, sand, still sand, and only sand, and sand, and sand again. The earth is so samely, that your eyes turn towards heaven—towards heaven, I mean, in sense of sky. You look to the sun for he is your taskmaster, and by him you know the measure of the work that you had done, and the measure of the work that remains for you to do. He comes when you strike your tent in the early morning, and then, for the first hour of the day, as you move forward on your camel, he stands at your near side, and makes you know that the whole day's toil is before you; then for a while, and a long while, you see him no more, for you are veiled and shrouded, and dare not look upon the greatness of his glory, but you know where he strides over head, by the touch of his flaming sword No words are spoken, but your Arabs moan, your camels sigh your skin glows, your shoulders ache, and for sights you see the pattern and the web of the silk that veils your eyes, and the glare of the outer light. Time labours on—your skin glows, your shoulders ache, your Arabs moan, your camels sigh, and you see the same pattern in the silk, and the same glare of light beyond; but conquering time marches on, and by and by the descending sun has compassed the heaven, and now softly touches your right arm, and throws your lank shadow over the sand right along on the way for Persia. Then again you look upon his face, for his power is all veiled in his beauty, and the redness of flames has become the redness of roses; the fair, wavy cloud that fled in the morning now comes to his sight once more — comes blushing—yet still comes on—comes burning with blushes, yet comes and clings to his side.

Then begins your season of rest. The world about you is all your own, and there, where you will, you pitch your solitary tent; there is no living thing to dispute your choice. Where at last the spot had been fixed upon and we came to a halt, one of the Arabs would touch the chest of my camel, and utter at the same time a peculiar gurgling sound. The beast instantly understood and obeyed the sign, and slowly sank under me, till she brought her body to a level with the ground: then gladly enough I alighted. The rest of the camels were unloaded and turned loose to browse upon the shrubs of the Desert, where shrubs there were, or where these faired, to wait for the small quantity of food that was allowed them out of our stores.

My servants, helped by the Arabs, busied themselves in pitching the tent and kindling the fire. Whilst this was doing I used to walk away towards the East, confiding in the print of my foot as a guide for my return. Apart from the cheering voices of my attendants, I could better know and feel that loneliness of the Desert. The influence of such scenes, however, was not of a softening kind, but filled me rather with a sort of children exaltation in the self-sufficiency which enabled me to stand thus alone in the wideness of Asia—a short-lived pride, for wherever man wanders, he still remains tethered by the chain that links him to his kind; and so when the night closed round me, I began to return—to return as it were to my own gate. Reaching at last some high ground I could see, and see with delight, the fire of our small encampment; and when, at last, I regained the spot, it seemed a very home that had sprung up for me in the midst of these solitudes. My Arabs were busy with their bread, — Mysseri rattling tea-cups, — the little kettle with her odd, oldmaidish looks sat humming away old songs about England, and two or three yards from the fire my tent stood prim and tight with open portal, and with welcoming look.

Sometimes in the earlier part of my journey the night breeze blew coldly; when that happened, the dry sand was heaped up outside round the skirts of the tent, and so the wind that everywhere else could sweep as he listed along those dreary plains, was forced to turn aside in his course for me. Then within my tent there were heaps of luxuries—dining-rooms, dressing-rooms, libraries, bedrooms, drawing-rooms, oratories, all crowded in the space of a hearth-rug. The first night, I remember, with my books and maps about me, I wanted a light. They brought me a taper, and immediately from out of the silent Desert there rushed in a flood of life, unseen before. Monsters of moths of all shapes and hues, that never before perhaps had looked upon the shining of a flame, now madly thronged into my tent, and dashed through the fire of the candle till they fairly extinguished it with their burning limbs. Those who had failed in attaining this martyrdom suddenly became serious, and clung despondingly to the canvas.

By and by there was brought to me the fragrant tea, and big masses of scorched and scorching toast, and the butter that had come all the way to me in this Desert of Asia, from out of that poor, dear, starving Ireland. I feasted like a king, — like four kings, — like a boy in the fourth form.

When the cold, sullen morning dawned, and my people began to load the camels. I always felt loath to give back to the waste this little spot of ground that had flowed for a while with the cheerfulness of a human dwelling. One by one the cloaks, the saddles, the baggages, the hundred things, that strewed the ground and made it look so familiar—all these were taken away, and laid upon the camels. A speck in the broad tracts of Asia remained still impressed with the mark of patent portmanteaus and the heels of London boots; the embers of the fire lay black and cold upon the sand; and these were the signs we left.

My tent was spared to the last, but when all else was ready for the start, then came its fall; the pegs were drawn, the canvas shivered, and in less than a minute there was nothing that remained of my genial home but only a pole and a bundle. The encroaching Englishman was off, and instant upon the fall of the canvas, like an owner who had waited and watched, the Genius of the Desert stalked in.

A. W KINGLAKE, *Eothen.*

A.W. Kinglake (1809-1891), historian of the Crimean War and author of *Eothen* (1844), one of the most brilliant and popular books of Eastern travel. *Eothen* takes its value not from any geographical, historical, or political information contained in it, but from the author's constantly and fully revealed personality, and from his vivid gift of communicating to the reader his own experience and impressions.

p. 1.04, 1. 2. ***made the most of about a pint of water.*** I washed myself as well as I could in a pint of water. The water was too precious to waste, and so only a pint was available for washing.

p. 104, 1. 24. ***valleys dug out....storm.*** The sand on the surface of the desert is always shifting, and winds which gather tremendous force there are able to dig out deep depressions in the sand.

p. 104, 1. 27. ***samely*** — a rare word = possessing a sameness, monotonous in appearance.

p. 105, 1. 10. ***veiled and shrouded.*** On account of the intense heat and glare travellers in the desert not only have to wear veils before their eyes, but wrap up the whole head and neck (shrouded).

p. 105, 1. 12. ***he strides....flaming sword.*** You know that the sun is shining (lit. moving) immediately over your head by the heat of his rays which penetrates even through your clothes.

p. 105, 1. 24. ***throws your lank shadow...for Persia.*** Lank = lengthened out. Kinglake was travelling south to Cairo, so that the sun setting in the west would cause a shadow of the travellers to be cast towards the east, in which direction by the road to Persia.

p. 105, 11. 26-31. ***his power all veiled...clings to his side.*** A beautiful passage descriptive of the colours of the sunset. The general meaning is: "The sun's power to burn and disappeared, and only his beauty remains: instead of seeming red-hot (the redness of flames), his orb is red in colour and beautiful like roses. The clouds which had appeared on the horizon at his rising, but were dissipated by his heat, appear once more in the cool of the evening and are coloured with red light (burning with blushes)."

p. 106, 11. 23-25. ***sort of childish exaltation... wideness of Asia.*** I felt a childish pride in my independence in being able to stand alone...; the feeling that he was able to exist in that wide desert if even for a short time without the need of help from others.

p. 107, 1.4. ***old maidish*** = the qualities associated with old unmarried ladies are primness, formality, and preciseness. The kettle—which forms such a strange contrast with its surroundings— suggests the formality of civilized life, but it is also actually has a prim appearance. The humming noise made by the water recalls to the traveller English home life—hence seems to be singing English songs.

p. 107, 1. 16. ***oratories.*** An oratory was a prayer-room or small chapel in old houses in England, usually built over the entrance.

p. 107, 1. 16. ***hearth-rug.*** The only luxury which he tent actually held was a small carpet of the size of the rug which England is spread before the fire-place. But he was in thoroughly content that it served him instead of all the luxurious apartments named.

p. 107, 1. 21. ***moths***= insects *(tituli)* which fly at night time.

p. 107, 1. 30. ***scorched and scorching toast.*** Toast bread held before a fire until it becomes scorched. The toast brought him was brought straight from the fire and was hot, so that it almost burned his mouth.

p. 107, 1. 32. ***poor, dear, starving Ireland.*** Ireland had always exported large quantities of farm produce, butter, eggs etc., even in times of depression and poverty.

p. 108, 1.2. ***a boy in the fourth form.*** In English public schools the fourth form is usually the last form below the Upper School. Boys of that and lower forms are proverbial for the love of eating.

p. 108, 1. 12. ***patent portmanteaus*** = large leather travelling bags or suitcases of a pattern patented by some manufacturer or other.

p. 108, 1. 23. ***the Genius of the Desert stalked in*** — Genius =the spirit. The Romans believed that special guardian spring or genii presided over rivers, lakes, mountains and localities generally: hence the use here. The meaning is that the spot where the camp had been became indistinguishable from the rest of the desert.

DAMASCUS

Damascus life begins very early in the morning, and the shops are almost all closed by one or two o'clock in the afternoon; thenceforth the cafés and gardens become filled, and, after sunset, you seldom meet anyone in the streets; the few who appear there are obliged to carry lanterns, and the different quarters of the town are enclosed by guarded gates.

I made the acquaintance of an Arab physician, who was possessed of considerable wealth, and was, moreover, a person of literary attainments. I accepted an invitation to visit him one evening; and, after traversing many silent streets, with guarded gates at either end, I arrived at one of the low and unpretending doorways I have mentioned.

I was admitted by a slave, and ushered through a long dark passage into a courtyard, which presented a very striking appearance; in the midst, the usual fountain leaped and sparkled in the rays that, falling from a painted lantern, converted each drop of spray into rubies or emeralds. Mimosas, hanging their flowery wreaths, and orange-trees bendi 'with their golden fruit, stood round, themselves, is owned by some tall luxuriant palms. On one side has any lights twinkled in the lattices of the hareem; on the other rose a wide alcove, with fretted roof, and a raised marble floor. The Divan was occupied by some gorgeously-clad, Turks, some merchants, and two Armenian priest in violent robes, and high black turbans. A large painted lantern threw its coloured light upon this picturesque and imposing group.

The circle, except the priests, rose as I entered, and remained standing until I had taken my seat; then, resuming theirs, each laid his hand upon his heart, and, bowing slowly, muttered a greeting. A pipe was then presented, and, according to the pleasant Eastern usage, no observation was addressed to me until I had time to become familiarized with the appearances that surrounded me.

My host was a noble-looking fellow, with piercing eyes and a long black beard; yet his countenance wore an expression of mirth and good-humour, that contrasted curiously with that reverend beard and lofty look. A long robe of dark flame-coloured silk was wrapped 'round his waist by a voluminous shawl, and a white Muslim turban was folded broadly on his forehead.

He held a conversion (through an interpreter) with great animation and interest on European topics, inquiring about steam, chemistry, and railways. When I observed that almost all our knowledge of chemistry and astronomy came originally from his country, he said that the Arab science was only spare *water* when it came to us in Frangistan" Yenifor fire under it and turn in into *steam.*"

The some conversation on medical subjects, he inquired very eagerly about magnetism, and begged that I would show him how it was done. Vainly I disclaimed any knowledge of the art; his enthusiasm on the subject was not be evaded, and, at last, I consented to explain the simple process.

He beckoned to a slave, who was standing by with folded arms, to approach; and, as the gaunt negro knelt before me, the whole circle closed round us, and looked on in breathless surprise, while I passed my hands slowly over my patient's eyes. Soon and suddenly, to my surprise and their astonishment, a shudder passed over the gigantic frame, and he sank upon the ground, huddled like a black cloak that had fallen from a peg. A low exclamation of "Wallah!" escaped from all the bystanders, who, one by one, endeavoured to waken him, but in vain. At length, they said quietly "He is dead," and resumed their pipes and their pleasant attitudes on the divans, as if it was all quite "regular". My host was beside himself with astonishment, and overwhelmed me with eager questions. The physician gazed in silence for sometime on the apparently breathless mass of humanity that lay heaped upon the floor; and then, with great diffidence and many apologies, requested I would bring him back to life, as he was worth nearly a hundred pounds. I was far from certain whether, or in what manner, thus was to be done, and postponed the attempt as long as possible. At length I tried, and succeeded with a vengeance!

It was like a thousand awakenings from a thing had or sleeps-long-suppressed consciousness seemed stream to flash upon his brain, too powerfully for its post endurance. With a fearful howl, he started to his feet, flung wide his arms, threw back his head, and, while his eyes rolled wildly in their sockets, he burst into a terrible shrieking sort of laughter. He seized a large vase of water, and dashed it into fragments on the marble floor: he tore up the divan, and smashed the lantern into a thousand bits; then, with his arms spread wide, he rushed about the courtyard, while the terrified Turks hid themselves, or fled in every direction. As I watched their horror-stricken countenances hurrying to and from in the various light of the moon and the remaining lantern, their long draperies tangling in the plants and pillars, their black pursuer stalking along as if engaged in some grim game of "blindman's buff"; together with the howl of the maniac ringing far and wide through the silent night, the shrieks of the women in the hareem above, the rapid tread of the pursued and the tramp of the pursuer among the palms and mimosas in the strange-looking courtyard, the whole seemed to me lie some fearful dream, of which I watched the result in painful and constrained suspense.

At length, the slave became exhausted by the violence of his emotions, and flinging himself upon the ground, sobbed as if his heart would break. Gradually he came to himself, looked puzzledly round on the scene of devastation he had wrought, and when quietly his meek attitude, and stood foulded arms on his naked chest.

I had preserved an air of quiet indifference (which I was far from feeling) through the transaction, the Orientals thought the matter was all quite right, and looked upon me with great respect. My host professed himself as much obliged as astonished by the performance, and begged of me to return the next evening to repeat the experiment. "Heaven forbid!" thought I, as I took leave of my host, as the following day I did of Damascus.

ELIOT WARBURTON, *The Crescent and the Cross.*

Eliot Warburton, the author of the book *The Crecent and the Cross,* from which this extract is taken was a friend of Kinglake and a fellow-traveller in Egypt.

p. 111, 1. 3. ***cafés*** — are restaurants in which coffee (whence the name) and refreshments generally are served. They are also places of general resort for the inhabitants: there they meet specially in the evening. In this respect in France and countries bordering on the Mediterranean they take the place of the English club.

p. 111, 1. 19. ***a painted lantern*** — an erection on the top of a room or dome fitted with windows of coloured glass to admit light. Painted lantern in the following paragraph has the ordinary sense of a lamp.

p. 111, 1. 20. ***Mimosas.*** Cf, note on p. 30, 1. 20.

p. 122, 1. 1. ***alcove*** = a recess in the wall of a room. A word of Arabic origin from *al gobbah*= the vault — a recess having usually a vaulted roof.

p. 112, 1. 1. ***with fretted roof,*** a carved roof.

p. 112, 1. 18. ***reverend beard*** - his beard gave him an air of gravity which commanded respect; his mirthful expression was a marked contrast to his otherwise venerable appearance.

p. 112, 1. 30. ***You put fire under it... steam.*** Referring to the discovery of the power of steam for driving engines.

p. 112, 1. 32. ***magnetism*** = an old name for hypnotism.

p. 113, 1. 18. ***"regular"*** = natural—what might be expected.

p. 113, 1. 28. ***with a vengeance*** - to a greater degree than was expected or desired.

p. 114, 1. 12. ***various light of the moon.*** The moon and the lantern were insufficient to light fully the whole of the apartment—parts of it were in light and parts in darkness.

p. 114, 1. 15. ***grim game of "blindman's buff."*** Blindman's buff is a children's game in which one child is blind-folded his object is to catch one of the other children; when he succeeds, the child who is caught in his turn has his eyes covered. The game here is described as grim because had the slave caught anyone he would probably have done him serious injury.

THE DEATH OF NELSON

It had been part of Nelson's prayer that the British Fleet might be distinguished by humanity in the victory which he expected. Setting an example himself, he twice gave orders to cease firing upon the "Redoubtable," supposing that she had struck because her great guns were silent; for as she carried no flag, there was no means of instantly ascertaining the fact. From this ship, which he had thus twice spared, he received his death. A ball fired from her mizentop, which, in the then situation of the two vessels, was not more than fifteen yards from that part of the deck where he was standing, struck the epaulette on his left shoulder, about a quarter after one, just in the heat of the action. He fell upon his face on the spot, which was covered with his poor secretary's blood. Hardy who was a few steps from him, turning round saw three men raising him up. "They have done for me at last, Hardy," said he. "I hope not~" cried Hardy. "Yes," he replied "my backbone is shot through." Yet even now, not for a moment losing his presence of mind, he observed, as they were carrying him down the ladder, that the tiller ropes, which had been shot away, were not yet replaced, and ordered that new ropes should be rove immediately; then, that he might not be seen by the crew, he took out his handkerchief and covered his face and his stars. Had he but concealed these badges of honour from the enemy, England, perhaps, would not have had cause to receive with sorrow the news of the Battle of Trafalgar.

The cockpit was crowded with wounded and dying men over whose bodies he was with some difficulty conveyed, and laid upon a pallet in the midshipman's berth. It was soon perceived upon examination that the wound was mortal. This, however, was concealed from all except captain Hardy, the chaplain, and the medical attendants. He himself being certain from the sensation on his back and the gush of blood which he felt momently within his breast that no human care could avail him; insisted that the surgeon should leave him, and attend to those to whom he might be useful. "For", said he, "you can do nothing for me." All that could be done was to fan him with paper, and frequently to give him lemonade, to allay his intense thirst. He was in great pain, and expressed much anxiety for the event of the action, which now began to declare itself. As often as a ship struck the crew of the Victory hurrahed, and at every hurrah a visible expression of joy gleamed in the eyes and marked the countenance of the dying hero. But he became impatient to see Captain Hardy, and as that officer, though often sent for, could not leave the deck, Nelson feared that some fatal cause prevented him, and repeatedly cried, "Will no one bring Hardy to me? He must be killed! He is surely dead!" An hour and ten minutes elapsed from the time when Nelson received his wound before Hardy could come to him. They shook hands in silence; Hardy in vain struggling to suppress the feelings of that most painful yet sublimest moment. "Well Hardy," said Nelson, "how goes the day with us?" "Very well," replied Hardy: "ten ships have struck, but five of their van have attacked, and show an intention of bearing down upon the Victory. I have called two or three of our fresh ships round, and I have no doubt of giving them a drubbing." "I hope," said Nelson, "none of our ships have struck." Hardy answered, "there was no fear of that." Then, and not till then, Nelson spoke of himself. "I am a dead man, Hardy," said he; "I am going fast; it will all be over with me soon. Come nearer to me. Let my dear Lady Hamilton have my hair, and all other things belonging to me." Hardy observed that he hoped Mr. Beatty could yet hold out some prospect of life. "Oh, no!" he replied, "it is impossible. My back is shot through. Beatty will tell you so." Captain Hardy then once more shook hands with him, and with a heart almost bursting hastened upon deck.

By this time all feeling below the breast was gone, and Nelson having made the surgeon ascertain this, said to him "You know I am gone. I know it. I feel something rising in my breast"— putting his hand on his left side — "which tells me so." And upon Beatty's inquiring whether his pain was very great? he replied, so great that he wished he was dead. "Yet," said he, in a lower voice, "one would like to live a little longer too!" And after a few minutes in the same undertone he added, "What would become of poor Lady Hamilton if she knew my situation?" Next to his country she occupied his thoughts. Captain Hardy, some fifty minutes after he had left the cock-pit, returned; and again taking the hand of his dying friend and commander congratulated him on having gained a complete victory. How many of the enemy were taken he did not know, as it was impossible to perceive them, distinctly; but fourteen or fifteen at least. "That's well," cried Nelson, "but I bargained for twenty." And then in a stronger voice he said "Anchor, Hardy, anchor." Hardy upon this hinted that Admiral Collingwood would take upon himself the direction of affairs. "Not while I live, Hardy!" said the dying Nelson, ineffectually endeavouring to raise himself from the bed' "do you anchor." His previous order for preparing to anchor had shown how clearly he foresaw the necessity of this. Presently, calling Hardy back, he said to him in a low voice, "Don't throw me overboard"; and he desired that he might be buried by his parents, unless it should please the king to order otherwise. Then reverting to private feelings. "Take care of my dear Lady Hamilton, Hardy. Kiss me, Hardy," said he. Hardy knelt down and kissed his cheek, and Nelson said, "Now I am satisfied. Thank God I have done my duty." Hardy stood over him in silence for a moment or two, then knelt again and kissed his forehead. "Who is that?" said Nelson; and being informed, he replied, "God bless you, Hardy." And Hardy then left him — for ever.

Nelson now desired to be turned on his right side, and said, "I wish I had not left the deck for I shall soon be gone." Death was indeed rapidly approaching. He said to the Chaplain,

"Doctor, I have not been a great sinner"; and after a short pause, "Remember that I leave Lady Hamilton and my daughter Horatia as a legacy to my country." His articulation now became difficult, but he was distinctly heard to say, "Thank God, I have done my duty!" These words he had repeatedly pronounced, and they were the last words which he uttered. He expired at thirty minutes after four, three hours and a quarter after he had received his wound.

R. SOUTHEY, *Life of Nelson.*

In youth a violent revolutionary, ***Southey*** (1774-1843) became an equally violent and equally sincere patriot with an eager admiration and enthusiasm for Nelson, his country's hero and defender from the navies of Napoleon. No biographer was more in sympathy with his hero than Southey. He designed his *Life of Nelson* as a manual "for the young sailor, which he may carry about with him," and he wrote it, therefore, in language that is studiously simple.

p. 117, 1. 2. ***humanity*** = consideration for the sufferings and feelings of the enemy.

p. 117, 1. 5. ***the 'Redoubtable."*** One of the French ships.

p. 117, 1. 5. ***struck.*** Struck (=hauled down) her colours — to haul down the flag was a sign that the ship had surrendered.

p. 117, 1. 10. ***mizentop.*** The mizen was the aftermost (hindmost) mast of the three in a three-masted ship. The top was the platform round the lower part of the mast. A gun was often planted upon it to fire down upon the enemy's deck.

p. 117, 1. 10. ***the then situation.*** This construction is only sparingly used by good writers of English. It should *not* be imitated whenever it can be avoided. Thus for "the then Viceroy" it is always possible to say 'the Viceroy of that time" or "of that period." It is never used in good English prose with the frequency that it appears in the composition of Indian students.

p. 117, 1. 13. ***epaulette*** — ornamental shoulder-piece forming part of the uniform of an admiral: formerly forming part also of an army officer's uniform.

p. 117, 1. 23. ***tiller ropes*** — the tiller is a lever fitted to the head of the rudder for steering; the ropes attached to either end of this lever are held by the man who steers the vessel.

p. 118, 1. 1. **rove** — past tense of "to reeve." A nautical term = to thread, to pass a rope through an aperture—the apertures in this case were at the end of the tiller.

p. 118, 1. 8. ***cockpit*** — the hinder part of a warship's lowest deck. The ships of Nelson's time had three decks. It was used in action as a hospital.

p. 118, 1. 10. ***pallet*** is a mattress, bed stuffed with straw.

p. 118, 1. 24. ***the event of the action....to declare itself*** = the result of the fight, which was now becoming clear—that is, it was evident that it would result in a victory for the English.

p. 119, 1. 6. ***sublimest*** = grandest, of a quality impressive in the highest degree—the word sublime suggests two qualities "grand and noble" and "awe-inspiring."

p. 119, 1. 9. ***van*** = the front line of ships.

p. 119, 1. 13. ***drubbing*** = a beating.

p. 119, 1. 18. ***Lady Hamilton*** — wife of Sir William Hamilton, to whom Nelson was devotedly attached.

p. 119, 1. 20, ***Beatty*** = surgeon or doctor on board the *Victory.*

p. 120, 1. 16. ***Admiral Collingwood*** — intimate friend of Nelson, and his immediate subordinate. On the death of his chief he succeeded to the command of the fleet.

p. 120, 1. 19. ***do you anchor*** — an emphatic command— "I order you to anchor."

DEATH OF SIR WALTER SCOTT

On Monday he remained in bed and seemed extremely feeble; but after breakfast on Tuesday the 17th (July 1832) he appeared revived somewhat, and was again wheeled about on the turf. Presently he fell asleep in his chair, and after dozing for perhaps half-an-hour, started awake, and shaking the plaids we had put about him from off his shoulders, said— "This is sad idleness. I shall forget what I have been thinking of, if I don't set it down now. Take me into my own room, and fetch the keys of my desk." He repeated this so earnestly that we could not refuse; his daughters went into his study, opened his writing-desk and laid paper and pens in the usual order, and I then moved him through the hall and into the spot where he had always been accustomed to work. When the chair was placed at his desk, and he found himself in the old position, he smiled and thanked us, and said— "Now give me my pen, and leave me for a little to myself." Sophia put the pen into his hand, and he endeavoured to close his fingers upon it, but they refused their office—it dropped on the paper. He sank back among his pillows, silent tears rolling down his cheeks; but composing himself by-and-by, motioned me to wheel him out of doors again. Laidlaw met us at the porch, and took his turn of the chair. Sir Walter, after a little while, again dropped into slumber. When he was awaking, Laidlaw said to me— "Sir Walter has had a little repose"— "No, Willie," said he— "no repose for Sir Walter but in the grave." The tears again rushed from his eyes. "Friends," said he, "don't let me expose myself — get me to bed—that's the only place."

With this scene ended our glimpse of daylight. Sir Walter never, I think, left his room afterwards, and hardly his bed, except for an hour or two in the middle of the day; and after another week he was unable even for this. During a few days he was in a state of painful irritation, and I saw realized all that he had himself prefigured in his description of the meeting between Crystal Croftangry and his paralytic friend. Dr. Ross came out from Edinburgh, bringing with him his wife, one of the dearest "nieces" of the Clerk's table. Sir Walter with some difficulty recognized the Doctor; but on hearing Mrs. Ross's voice, exclaimed at once— "Isn't that Kate Hume?" These kind friends remained for two or three days with us. Clarkson's lancet was pronounced necessary, and the relief it afforded was, I am happy to say, very effectual.

After this he declined daily, but still there was great strength to be wasted, and the process was long. He seemed, however, to suffer no bodily pain, and his mind, though hopelessly obscured, appeared, when there was any symptom of consciousness, to be dwelling, with rare exceptions, on serious and solemn things; the accent of the voice grave, sometimes awful, but never querulous, and very seldom indicative of any angry or resentful thought. Now and then he imagined himself to be administering justice as Sheriff: and once or twice he seemed to be ordering Tom Purdie about trees. A few times also, I am sorry to say, we could perceive that his fancy was at Jedburgh, and "Burk Sir Walter" escaped him in a melancholy tone. But commonly whatever we could follow him in was a fragment of the Bible (especially the Prophecies of Isaiah and the Book of Job)— or some petition in the litany—or a verse of some psalm (in the old Scottish metrical versions), or of some of the magnificent hymns of the Romish ritual, in which he had always delighted, but which probably hung on his memory now in connection with the Church services he had attended while in Italy. We very often heard distinctly the cadence of the "Dies Irae"; and I think the very last stanza that we could make out was the first of a still greater favourite:

"Stabat Mater dolorosa
Juxta crucem lachrymosa
Dum pendebat filius."

All this time he continued to recognize his daughters, Laidlaw, and myself, whenever we spoke to him—and received every attention with a most touching thankfulness. Mr. Clarkson, too, was always saluted with the old courtesy, though the cloud opened but a moment for him to do so. Most truly might it be said that the gentleman survived the genius.

As I was dressing on the morning of Monday the 17th of

September, Nicholson came into my room, and told me that his master had awoke in a state of composure and consciousness, and wished to see me immediately. I found him entirely himself, though in the last extreme of feebleness. His eye was clear and calm—every trace of the wild fire of delirium extinguished. "Lockhart," he said, "I may have but a minute to speak to you. My dear, be a good man—be virtuous—be religious—be a good man. Nothing else will give you any comfort when you come to lie here." —He paused, and I said—"Shall I send for Sophia and Anne?"-- "No," he said, "don't disturb them. Poor souls! I know they were up all night—God bless you all." With this he sank into a very tranquil sleep, and, indeed, he scarcely afterwards gave any sign of consciousness, except for an instant on the arrival of his sons. They, on learning that the scene was about to close, obtained a new leave of absence from their posts, and both reached Abbotsford on the 19th. About half past one p.m. on the 21st of September, Sir Walter breathed his last, in the presence of all his children. It was a beautiful day—to warm that every window was wide open—and to perfectly still that the sound of all others most delicious to his ear, the gentle ripple of the Tweed over its pebbles, was distinctly audible as we knelt around the bed, and his eldest son kissed and closed his eyes.

J. G. LOCKHART, *Life of Scott.*

J. G. Lockhart (1794-1854), the friend and son-in-law of Sir Walter Scott, was no less than Southey in perfect sympathy with his hero. The closing chapter of his *Life of Scott* are probably unequalled in biographical literature. No more moving and yet restrained and dignified picture of the decay and death of a great man has ever been written.

p. 124, 1. 6. ***plaids.*** Scotch shawls of cloth, usually brightly coloured like the kilt or uniform of a Highland regiment.

p. 124, 1. 14. ***I***=Lockhart, the writer of this biography.

p. 124, 1. 19. ***Sophia.*** Sir Walter Scott's daughter.

p. 125, 1. 1. ***Laidlaw.*** Laidlaw was a kind of estate manager for Scott; he was both servant and friend.

p. 125, 1. 2. ***took his turn of the chair***==*took his turn in wheeling the chair.*

p. 125, 11. 16-18. ***he had himself prefigured......paralytic friend.*** Crystal Croftangry is a character in one of Scott's short stories in the *Chronicles of the Canongate,* who after an absence of many years visits an old friend, only to find him paralysed and decayed in body and in mind. Scott's present condition proved the insight and the accuracy of this description of this old man.

p. 125, 1. 20. ***the Clerk's table.*** Clerk==Chief Justice Clerk—a Scottish legal rank.

p. 125, 1. 22. Kate Hume—the maiden name of Mrs. Ross.

p. 125, 1. 24. ***Clarkson's lancet.*** Clarkson was Scott's family doctor. The lancet was used in the letting of blood.

p. 126, 1. 5. ***Sheriff.*** Scott had been appointed Sheriff of Selkirkshire (a country in Scotland) in 1799. The Sheriff is the chief legal officer of a shire or country.

p. 126, 1. 6. ***Tom Purdie.*** A faithful and valued friend and servant who had recently died. In 1804 Purdie had been brought before the Sheriff on a charge of poaching, but Scott was so touched by the pathos and humour of his defence that instead of punishing him he took into his service, first a shepherd and then as forester.

p. 126, 1.8. ***Jedburgh......Burk Sir Walter.*** This refers to an unpleasant experience during the parliamentary election of 1831 at Jedburgh, a small town in Scotland not far from Abbotsford, whither Scott had gone to give his support to the Tory or Conservative candidate. Political passion ran high, and the radical mob raised the cry, "Burk (murder) Sir Walter." Burk is derived from Burke, a notorious murderer who was changed in Edinburgh in 1829.

p. 126, 1.12. ***the litany***=a part of the service of the church consisting of a series of petitions addressed to the Deity, in which the minister and the congregation take alternate parts.

p. 126, 1. 13. ***in the old Scottish metrical version.*** The psalms sung in Scottish churches are, unlike the versions in the Anglican prayer-book, in metre and rhyme.

p. 126, 1. 15. ***Romish ritual***=the services used in the Roman Catholic Church: in them ceremonial (the performances of rites and ceremonies) plays a large part; ritual=ceremonial.

p. 126, 1. 17. ***while in Italy.*** Scott set out for Italy in 1831 in the hope of recovering his shattered health: but he returned to Scotland in the following year only to die.

p. 126, 1. 18. *cadence*—rhythm—literally "the fall of the voice at the end of a song"--then "the rise and fall": so "the rhythm."

p. 126, 1. 19. ***Dies Irae***—a famous Latin hymn on "the day of wrath"=the Day of Judgment. Scott has translated it in the *Lay of the Last Minstrel.*

p. 126, 1. 22. ***Stabat Mater***=another hymn relating the feelings of Mary the mother of Christ at beholding her Son's sufferings on the Cross. The three lines may be roughly translated as follows:

"O'ercome with tears, oppressed with grief,

Besides the Cross the Mother stood

While her Son hung (on the Cross)."

p. 126, 1.30. ***though the cloud opened......do so.*** Though his brain became clear only long enough to enable him to recognise Mr. Clarkson and salute him.

p. 126, 1.32. ***the gentleman survived the genius***—the instincts of a gentleman, which Scott possessed in a strong degree remained with him after his imagination (the characteristic of a genius) had ceased to operate. He showed no signs during his last hours of the genius he had possessed.

p. 127, 1.2. ***Nicholson.*** Scott's valet or personal servant.

p. 127, 1.27. ***the Tweed*** — the river flows close to Abbotsford; the sound the water makes as it passes over the pebbles which form its bed as a peculiar charm.

THE TAKING OF QUEBEC

For full two hours the procession of boats, borne on the current, steered silently down the St. Lawrence. The stars were visible, but the night was moonless and sufficiently dark. The General was in one of the foremost boats, and near him was a young midshipman, John Robinson, afterwards Professor of Natural Philosophy in the University of Edinburgh. He used to tell in his later life how Wolfe, in a low voice, repeated Gray's "Elegy in a Country Churchyard" to the officers about him. Probably it was to relieve the intense strain of his thoughts. Among the rest was the verse which his own fate was soon to illustrate:

"The paths of glory lead but to the grave."

"Gentlemen," he said as his recital ended, "I would rather have written those lines than take Quebec."

As they neared their destination the tide bore them in towards the shore and the mighty wall of rock and forest towered in darkness on their left. The dead stillness was suddenly broken by the sharp "Qui Vive!" of a French sentry, invisible in the thick gloom. "France!" answered a Highland officer from one of the boats of the light infantry. He had served in Holland and spoke French fluently.

"A quel regiment?"

"Dela Reine," replied the Highlander. He knew that a part of that corps was with Boungainville. The sentry expecting the convoy of provisions from that commander, was satisfied, and did not ask for the password.

Soon after, the foremost boats were passing the heights of Samos, when another sentry challenged them, and they could see him through the darkness running down to the edge of the water within range of a pistol-shot. In answer to his questions the same officer replied, in French: "Provision boats. Don't make a noise; the English will hear us." In fact, the sloop-of-war Hunter was anchored in the stream not far off. This time, again, the sentry let them pass. In a few moments they rounded the headland above the Anse de Foulon. There was no sentry there. The strong current swept the boats of the light infantry a little below the intended landing-place. They disembarked on a narrow strand at the foot of heights as steep as a hill covered with trees can be. The twenty-four volunteers led the way, climbing with what silence they might, closely followed by a much larger body.

Montcalm was amazed at what he saw. He had expected a detachment, and he had found an army. Full in sight before him stretched the lines of Wolfe: the close ranks of the English infantry, a silent wall of red, and the wild array of the Highlanders, with their waving tartans, and bagpipes screaming defiance.

It was towards ten o'clock when from the high ground on the right of the line, Wolfe saw that the crisis was near. The French on the ridge had formed themselves into three bodies, regulars in the centre, regulars and Canadians on right and left. Two field pieces, which had been dragged up the heights, fired on them with grape-shot, and the British troops, rising from the ground, prepared to receive them. In a few moments more they were in motion. They came on rapidly uttering loud shouts, and firing as soon as they were within range. Their ranks, ill ordered at the best, were further confused by a number of Canadians who had been mixed among the regulars, and who, after hastily firing, threw themselves on the ground to reload. The British advanced a few rods, then halted and stood still. When the French were within forty paces the word of command rang out, and a crash of musketry answered all along the line. The volley was delivered with remarkable precision. In the battalions of the centre, which had suffered least from the enemy's bullets, the simultaneous explosion was afterwards said by the French officers to have sounded like a cannon-shot. Another volley followed, and then a furious clattering fire that lasted but a minute or two. When the smoke rose a miserable sight was revealed: the ground cumbered with dead and wounded, the advancing masses stopped short and turned into a frantic mob, shouting, cursing, gesticulating. The order was given to charge. Then over the field rose the British cheer, mixed with the fierce yell of the Highland slogan. Some of the corps pushed forward with the bayonet; some advanced firing. The clansmen drew their broadswords and dashed on, keen and swift as bloodhounds. At the English right, though the attacking column was broken to pieces, a fire was still kept up, chiefly it seems, by sharpshooters from the bushes and cornfields, where they had lain for an hour or more. Here Wolfe himself led the charge at the head of the Louisbourg, grenadiers A shot shattered his wrist. He wrapped his handkerchief about it and kept on. Another shot struck him, and he still advanced, when a third lodged in his breast. He staggered, and sat on the ground. Lieutenant Brown, of the grenadiers; one Henderson, a volunteer in the same company; and a private soldier, aided by an officer of artillery who ran to join them, carried him in their arms to the rear. He begged them to lay him down. They did so, and asked if he would have a surgeon. "There is no need," he answered, "it is all over with me." A moment after, one of them cried out, "They run; see how they run!" "Who run?" Wolfe demanded, like a man roused from sleep. "The enemy, Sir. They give way everywhere." "Go, one of you, to Colonel Burton," returned the dying man; "tell him to march Webb's regiment down to Charles River, to cut off their retreat from the bridge!" Then, turning on his side, he murmured,"Now, God be praised, I will die in peace!" and in a few moments his gallant soul had fled.

FRANCIS PARKMAN, *Montcalm and Wolfe*

Parkman (1823-1893) is at once a master of narrative and picturesque history, and a lover of truth for whom no pains were too great that might establish a fact. He tells us that he wrote as a sharer or spectator of the actions he described. The passage selected is from his *Montcalm and Wolfe,* the dramatic story of the great contest between England and France for possession of

Canada.

p. 131, 1.2. ***St. Lawrence.*** The river in Canada on which Quebec stands: the town is situated on a lofty ridge knows as the Heights of Abraham.

p. 131, 1.9. ***Gray's "Elegy in a Country Churchyard."*** Thomas Gray (1716-71) wrote this famous poem in 1751.

p. 131, 1. 21. **"Qui Vive!"** equivalent to the English "Who goes there?": the challenge used by sentries.

p. 132, 1.1. ***"A quel regiment?"***=="To what regiment (do you belong)?"

p. 132, 1.2. ***"De la Reine"***=="The Queen's (Regiment)."

p. 132, 1.3. ***Bougainville*** (1729-1811)=French navigator and soldier, at this time aide-de-camp to Montcalm.

p. 132, 1.17. ***Anse de Foulan.*** A tiny landing-place on the river a mile and a half above Quebec, now called Wolfe's Cove.

p. 132, 1.25. ***Montcalm*** (1712-1759), the brilliant and gallant general who commanded the French force in Canada. He fell mortally wounded in the action described in this passage.

p. 132, 1.30. ***tartans.*** The kilts worn by Highland regiments.

p. 133, 1.5. ***field pieces***=light guns, easily moved about.

p. 133, 1.6. ***grape-shot.*** A number of small balls enclosed in a bag so that when fired the balls would scatter.

p. 133, 1.24. ***a clattering fire.*** Firing which produced an irregular, confused sound.

p. 133, 1.31. ***slogan***—the Highland war-cry.

p. 133, 1.32. **pushed forward**=advanced hurriedly.

p. 134, 1.5. ***sharpshooters***--especially skilled marksmen Scotia names after the King of France. Under French rule was second only to Quebec in importance.

p. 134, 1.25. ***Charles River.*** The Charles River runs into the St. Lawrence from the north immediately to the east of Quebec.

ST. FRANCIS OF ASSISI

ST. FRANCIS was born in the romantic town of Assisi, of a family, the Bernardini, engaged in trade. His birth took place while his father was on a mercantile journey in France; on his return his new-born son was baptized by the name of Francis. His mother, Picca, loved him with all a mother's tenderness for her first-born. He received the earliest rudiments of instruction from the clergy of the parish of St. George: he was soon taken to assist his father in his trade. The father, a hard money-making man, was shocked at first by the vanity and prodigality of his son. The young Francis gave banquets to his juvenile friends, dressed splendidly, and the streets of Assisi rang with the songs and revels of the joyous crew; but even then his bounty to the poor formed a large part of his generous wastefulness. He was taken captive in one of the petty wars which had broken out between Perugia and Assisi, and remained a whole year in prison. He as then seized with a violent illness; when he rose from his bed nature looked cold and dreary; he began to feel disgust of the world. The stirrings of some great but yet undefined purpose were already awake within him. He began to see visions, but as yet they were of war and glory: the soldier was not dead in his heart. He determined to follow the fortunes of a youthful poor knight who was setting out to fight under the banner of the "Gentle Count," Walter of Brienne, against the hated Germans. At Spoleto he again fell ill; his feverish visions took another turn.

Francis now felt upon him that profound religious thraldom which he was never to break, never to desire to break. His whole soul became deliberately, calmly, ecstatic faith. He began to talk mysteriously of his future bride—that bride was Poverty. He resolved never to refuse alms to a poor person. He found his way to Rome, threw down all he possessed, no costly offering, on the altar of St. Peter.

On his return he joined a troop of beggars, and exchanged his dress for the rags of the filthiest among them. His mother heard and beheld all his strange acts with a tender and prophetic admiration. To a steady trader like the father it was folly if not madness. He was sent with a valuable bale of goods to sell at Foligno. On his return he threw all the money down at the feet of the priest of St. Damian to rebuild his church, as well as the price of his horse, which he likewise sold. The priest refused the gift. In the eyes of the father this was dishonesty as well as folly.

Francis concealed himself in a cave, where he lay hid for a month in solitary prayer. He returned to Assisi, looking so wild and haggard, that the rabble hooted him as he passed, and pelted him with mire and stones. The gentle Francis appeared to rejoice in every persecution. The indignant father shut him up in a dark chamber, from which, after a time, he was released by the tender solicitude of his mother.

Bernardini now despaired of his unprofitable and intractable son, whom he suspected of alienating other sums besides that which he had received for the cloth and the horse. He cited him before the magistrates to compel him to abandon all rights on his patrimony, which he was disposed to squander in this thriftless manner. Francis declared that he was a servant of God, and declined the jurisdiction of the civil magistrate. The cause came before the Bishop. The Bishop earnestly exhorted Francis to yield up to his father any money which he might possess, or to which he was entitled. "It might be ungodly gain, and so unfit to be applied to holy uses." "I will give up the very clothes I wear," replied the enthusiast, encouraged by the gentle demeanour of the Bishop. He stripped himself entirely naked. "Peter Bernardini was my father: I have now but one Father, He that is in Heaven." The audience burst into tears; the Bishop threw his mantle over him and ordered, an old coarse dress of an artisan to be brought: he then received Francis into his service.

Francis was not wedded to Poverty; but Poverty he would only love in its basest form—mendicancy. He wandered abroad, was ill-used by robbers; on his escape received from an old friend a hermit's attire—a short tunic, a leathern girdle, a staff and slippers. He begged at the gates of monasteries; he discharged the most menial offices. With even more profound devotion he dedicated himself for some time in the hospital at Gubbio to the lepers. He tended them with more than necessary affectionateness, washed their feet, dressed their sores, and is said to have wrought miraculous cures among them.

On his return to Assisi he employed himself in the restoration of the Church of St. Damian. "Whoever will give me one stone shall have one prayer; whoever two, two; three, three." The people mocked, but Francis went on carrying the stones in his own hands, and the church began to rise. He refused all food which he did not obtain by begging. His father reproached him and uttered his malediction. He took a beggar of the basest class: "Be thou my father and give me thy blessing." But so successful was he in awakening the charity of the inhabitants of Assisi, that not only the Church of St. Damian but two others, through his means arose out of their ruins to decency and even splendour. One day in Church he heard the text, "Provide neither gold, nor silver, nor brass in your purses. Neither scrip for your journey, neither two coats, neither shoes nor yet staves." He threw away his wallet, his staff, and his shoes, put on the coarsest dark grey tunic, bound himself with a cord, and set out through the city calling all to repentance.

This strange but fervent piety of Francis could not but, in that age, kindle the zeal of others. Wonder grew into admiration, admiration into emulation, emulation into a blind following of his footsteps. Disciples, one by one, began to gather round him. He retired with them to a lonely spot in the bend of the river, called Rivo Torto.

H. H. MILMAN, *Latin Christianity.*

No Indian student can fail to see the beauty of the life and character of St. Francis of Assisi. His ascetic ideal and practice, his devotion to the poor, the sick, and the leper, his love of poverty, his feeling for the kinship of all living things, which led him to preach to the birds and the fishes, have always been considered in India the essential saintly virtues. The Franciscan order of preaching friars, whose members are to be found in every corner of the world leading self-sacrificing lives, was founded by St. Francis in 1209. *Latin Christianity,* by Dean Milman (1791-1868), is noteworthy for its reverent yet human presentation of the great ascetic saints of the medieval Catholic Church.

p. 137, 1. 8. ***parish.*** A parish is a subdivision of a county or a town having its own church, with one or more of clergymen attached to it.

p. 137, 1. 18. ***Perugia and Assisi*** are neighbouring towns in Umbria, a province in Central Italy.

p. 137, 1. 20. ***nature looked cold and dreary.*** The world no longer seemed to be the pleasant and cheerful place he had thought it to be before his illness. This illness altered his whole outlook upon life.

p. 137, 1. 22. ***The stirrings of some great......within him.*** He began to feel that he was born to carry out some great mission, but he was as yet uncertain of what nature it was to be.

p. 138, 1. 1. ***the soldier was not dead in his heart.*** His love of the soldier's profession was still strong in him.

p. 138, 1. 4. ***Walter of Brienne***=Count of Brienne in the N.E. of France.

p. 138, 1. 5. ***Spoleto***==a town also in Umbria.

p. 138, 1. 7. **religious thraldom.** The strong binding power of religion upon his mind.

p. 138, 1. 14. ***altar of St. Peter.*** At the altar in the great Church of St. Peter's at Rome. The rebuilding of St. Peter's began in 1450 and the church was consecrated in November 1626.

p. 138, 1. 22. ***Foligno.*** Another town in Umbria, south of Assisi.

p. 138, 1. 23. ***St. Damian.*** A church in Assisi.

p. 139, 1. 6. ***alienating***—removing, abstracting.

p. 139, 1. 13. ***The cause came before the Bishop.*** The Bishops held ecclesiastical courts in medieval times, which tried all cases in which the clergy were involved. As this case concerned a church Francis claimed that it should come under the Bishop's jurisdiction.

p. 139, 1. 28. ***its basest form.*** In its humblest, lowliest form.

p. 140, 1. 1. ***offices***—duties.

p. 140, 1. 3. ***Gubbio***-—a town in Umbria, north of Perugia.

p. 140, 1. 23. ***scrip.*** A beggar's or pilgrim's wallet or bag.

MY FIRST OUTING

Once, when the dengue fever was raging in Calcutta, some portion of our extensive family had to take shelter in Chhatu Babu's river-side villa. We were among them.

This was my first outing. The bank of the Ganges welcomed me into its lap like a friend of a former birth. There, in front of the servants' quarters, was a grove of Guava trees; and, sitting in the verandah under the shade of these, gazing at the flowing current through the gaps between their trunks, my days would pass. Every morning, as I awoke, I somehow felt the day coming to me like a new gilt-edged letter, with some unheard-of news awaiting me on the opening of the envelop. And, lest I should lose my fragment of it, I would hurry through my toilet to my chair outside. Every day there was the ebb and flow of the tide on the Ganges; the various gait of so many different boats; the shifting of the shadows of the trees from west to east; and, over the fringe of shade-patches of the woods on the opposite bank, the gush of golden life-blood through the pierced breast of the evening sky. Some days would be cloudy from early morning; the opposite woods black; black shadows moving over the river. Then with a rush would come the vociferous rain, blotting out the horizon; the dim line of the other bank taking its leave in tears; the river swelling with suppressed heavings; and the moist wind making free with the foliage of the trees overhead.

I felt that out of the bowels or wall, beam and rafter, I had a new birth into the outside. In making fresh acquaintance with things, the dingy covering of petty habits seemed to drop off the world. I am sure that the sugar cane molasses, which I had with cold "luchis" for my breakfast, could not have tasted different from the ambrosia which Indira quaffs in his heaven; for, the immortality is not in the nectar but in the taster, and thus is missed by those who seek it.

Behind the house was a walled-in enclosure with a tank and a flight of steps leading into the water from a bathing platform. On one side of the platform was an immense Jambolan tree, and all round were various fruit trees, growing in thick clusters, in the shade of which the tank nestled in its privacy. The veiled beauty of this retried little inner garden had a wonderful charm for me, so different from the broad expanse of the river-bank in front. It was like the bride of the house, in the seclusion of her mid-day siesta, resting on a many-coloured quilt of her own embroidering, murmuring low the secrets of her heart. Many a mid-day hour did I spend alone under that Jambolan tree dreaming of the fearsome kingdom of the Yakshas within the depths of the tank.

I had a great curiosity to see a Bengal village. Its clusters of cottages, its thatched pavilions, its lanes and bathing places, its games and gatherings, its fields and markets, its life as a whole as I saw it in my imagination, greatly attracted me. Just such a village was right on the other side of our garden wall, but it was forbidden to us. We had come out, but not into freedom. We had been in a cage, and were now on a perch, but the chain was still there.

One morning two of our elders went out for a stroll into the village. I could not restrain my eagerness any longer, and, slipping out unperceived, followed them for some distance. As I went along the deeply shaded lane, with its close thorny "seora" hedges, by the side of the tank covered with green water weeds, I rapturously took in picture after picture. I still remember the man with the bare body, engaged in a belated toilet on the edge of the tank, cleaning his teeth with the chewed end of a twig. Suddenly my elders became aware of my presence behind them. "Get away, get away, go back at once!" they scolded. They were scandalized. My feet were bare, I had no scarf or upper robe over my tunic, I was not dressed fit to come out; as if it was my fault! I never owned any socks or superfluous apparel, so not only went back disappointed for that morning, but had no chance of repairing my short-comings and being allowed to come out any other day. However, though the Beyond was thus shut out from behind, in front the Ganges freed me from all bondage, and my mind, whenever, it listed, could embark on the boats gaily sailing along, and hie away to lands not named in any geography.

This was forty years ago. Since then I have never set foot again in that "Champak"--shaded villa garden. The same old house and the same old tree must still be there, but I know it cannot any longer be the same—for where am I now to get that fresh feeling of wonder which made it what it was?

We returned to our Jorasanko house in town. All my days were as so many mouthfuls offered up to be gulped down into the yawning interior of the Normal School.

RABINDRANATH TAGORE, *My Reminiscences.*

Dr. Rabindranath Tagore's prose is noteworthy for its wealth of poetic imagery. The last portion of this passage is however, simple, and the whole is a sympathetic and vivid picture of river scenery in Bengal.

p. 143, 1. 1. ***dengue fever***=an infectious fever causing severe pain in the joints.

p. 143, 1. 13. ***gilt-edged letter***=such as are used for sending invitations to marriages.

p. 143, 1. 18. ***various gait***=each boat in motion presented a different appearance.

p. 143, 1. 20. ***over the fringe of shade-patches....evening sky.*** The poet is looking at the scenery of the opposite bank of the river. The woods are evidently at some distance and form a fringe (thin irregular border) of shadow against the sky-line from rifts in the clouds emerge shafts of golden light.

p. 144, 1. 3. ***the dim line......in tears***=the falling rain made it impossible for you to see the line of the opposite bank.

p. 144, 1. 5. ***making free with***=moving violently.

p. 144, 1. 7. ***I felt that out of the bowels........into the outside.*** I felt that during my stay in this villa (wall, beam and rafter) I was getting a new insight into life.

p. 144, 1. 13. ***ambrosia***=the food eaten by gods; nectar, their drink. Both words are of Greek origin.

p. 144, 1. 14. ***immortality is not in the nectar......seek it.*** To see beauty and truth one must be born with the power to see it: it will not come by seeking.

p. 144, 1. 27. ***siesta***==mid-day rest.

p. 146, 1.4. ***champak***=the *champa* tree.

p. 146, 1.10. ***All my days were so many mouthfuls....... Normal School***=all my days were spoiled for me by being spent at school.

